angel
WISDOM

angel

WISDOM

Bring the Guidance of Angels

into Your Life

GLENNYCE S. ECKERSLEY

& GARY QUINN

JEREMY P. TARCHER/PENGUIN

a member of Penguin Group (USA) Inc.

New York

JEREMY P. TARCHER/PENGUIN
Published by the Penguin Group
Penguin Group (USA) Inc., 375 Hudson Street, New York, New York 10014, USA •
Penguin Group (Canada), 90 Eglinton Avenue East, Suite 700, Toronto, Ontario M4P 2Y3,
Canada (a division of Pearson Canada Inc.) • Penguin Books Ltd, 80 Strand, London
WC2R 0RL, England • Penguin Ireland, 25 St Stephen's Green, Dublin 2, Ireland
(a division of Penguin Books Ltd) • Penguin Group (Australia), 250 Camberwell Road,
Camberwell, Victoria 3124, Australia (a division of Pearson Australia Group Pty Ltd) • Penguin
Books India Pvt Ltd, 11 Community Centre, Panchsheel Park, New Delhi—110 017, India •
Penguin Group (NZ), 67 Apollo Drive, Rosedale, North Shore 0632, New Zealand (a division
of Pearson New Zealand Ltd) • Penguin Books (South Africa) (Pty) Ltd, 24 Sturdee Avenue,
Rosebank, Johannesburg 2196, South Africa

Penguin Books Ltd, Registered Offices: 80 Strand, London WC2R 0RL, England

Most Tarcher/Penguin books are available at special quantity discounts for bulk purchase for
sales promotions, premiums, fund-raising, and educational needs. Special books or book
excerpts also can be created to fit specific needs. For details, write Penguin Group (USA) Inc.
Special Markets, 375 Hudson Street, New York, NY 10014.

Library of Congress Cataloging-in-Publication Data

Eckersley, Glennyce S.
Angel wisdom : bring the guidance of angels into your life / Glennyce S. Eckersley & Gary
Quinn.—1st American ed.
p.   cm.
ISBN 978-1-58542-702-4
1. Angels.   I. Quinn, Gary.   II. Title.
BL477.E24   2008   2008039070
202'.15—dc22

Printed in the United States of America
1   3   5   7   9   10   8   6   4   2

BOOK DESIGN BY NICOLE LAROCHE

To the Angels who bless us with divine energies,
Who revitalize our minds, bodies, and spirits,
Who teach us love, compassion, and honor,
Enabling us to heal the Earth and each other.

ᴐ contents ᴄ

Introduction *xi*

1. angels of guidance *1*

2. angels of healing *17*

3. angels of wisdom *33*

4. angels of joy and laughter *53*

5. angels of perception *81*

6. angels of color and light *113*

7. angels of love *143*

Epilogue *163*
Acknowledgments *165*

∽ introduction ∼

ANGELS AROUND THE WORLD

We have all heard of angels, those marvelous celestial beings who bring messages from on high, who offer warnings in times of danger, who tender healing and comfort in times of need, and who even bring enlightenment to a privileged few. Throughout the centuries, earthbound humans have been obsessed with the concept of flight and the desire to reach other worlds and dimensions, and so have been fascinated by angels. Around the globe, people have always spoken of angels, written about them, composed poems and sung about them. Artists have painted angels, sculptors have fashioned them and they feature in virtually every major world religion. Although indigenous peoples and ancient civilizations may have known these spiritual beings by different names, their artworks too clearly depict angels.

If we consider history in relation to angels, a pattern emerges. In times of dramatic events associated with the world's great religions, wars, natural disasters, and even in times of devastating disease, we find a sharp increase in recorded angel sightings. Clearly, in times of great stress people have always turned to God and His angels.

Ancient peoples accepted the presence and purpose of angels without question. But, as societies have grown in sophistication over the centuries, people have become less and less inclined to acknowledge spiritual intervention in their lives. This is particularly true of the last century, when science and materialism appeared to hold sway over our hearts and souls. Western society certainly seemed to have lost its way spiritually: it was as if we had lost the ability to commit to the concept of a Higher Source. The new millennium, however, has happily brought renewed interest in all aspects of spirituality and a willingness in people to talk openly about their angelic experiences.

Recent times may have seen angels suffer from a slightly saccharine image, depicting them as fluffy beings perched precariously on top of Christmas trees, for example, but this trivializes their true nature. As you will discover in these pages, true angelic appearance can vary immensely—from a normal-looking person in everyday dress to an awesome traditional angel. And these magical beings do not appear on hallowed ground alone but walk among us in our everyday lives. They assume the guise necessary for each occasion, to suit each individual's needs.

HOW CAN ANGELS HELP YOU?

In this book, we—authors Glennyce and Gary—have teamed up to help you develop your personal relationship with the angels. We have both enjoyed many years of working with angels as our inspiration, each of us developing a special relationship with them. Glennyce has researched angels and other spiritual phenomena for the past decade, and will enthrall you with wonderful true stories from around the globe. Gary will give you the practical tools and spiritual exercises to help you to communicate with angels and to develop your spiritual contact with these heavenly beings.

Angel Wisdom is divided into seven chapters, each with a particular theme relating to the ways in which angels can appear in our lives. The stories will show you how angels have helped others, and also teach you how to look out for telltale signs that may help you to connect with angels yourself. Powerful blessings and affirmations will help you learn how to be receptive to these celestial beings and how to accept their help as it is offered.

The chapters also include Divine Keys to help you to increase your awareness and balance your energies. The Divine Keys will enable you to create transformation in your life. They will carry you from any situation or mind-set, such as from fear to love, helping you to release anything that is less than a higher loving thought and enabling you to understand that you yourself are no less than a complete expression of infinite intelligence.

SOME SIMPLE TECHNIQUES TO GET YOU STARTED

As you will discover in the stories in this book, angelic power can protect you, guide you, and strengthen your connection

with the Higher Source. Whatever your age or your personal
background, angels will be ready to work with you at all times.
Whether you would like to create the perfect job or relationship, or improve your health, you can access your angelic
guides by learning to listen to your true inner voice—which
is the key to everything. A positive attitude and willingness
to change also make for a strong starting point. By changing
your old patterns from within, and refocusing your energy in
a positive way, you will start to see changes manifest in your
life almost immediately—but you must trust this process and
allow it to unfold.

Here is a simple technique to help you tune into your
inner voice and begin to access your own angelic
guides:

STEP 1. Sit in a quiet place where you are
unlikely to be disturbed. Clear your mind, letting unwanted thoughts drift by, and relax your
body.

STEP 2. Breathe in deeply several times. Now
speak to your angelic guides out loud: I call upon
my higher angelic guides for complete protection
and answers. Repeat this.

STEP 3. Concentrate your gaze on your hands,
welcoming your angelic guides into your body
and mind.

STEP 4. In your mind, formulate a clear question that you would like your guides to answer. Be receptive to whatever comes into your thoughts, allowing your guides to bring you the perfect answer to your question.

AFFIRMATIONS, PRAYERS, AND BLESSINGS

Simple affirmations, prayers, and blessings can also play an important part in helping you to connect to your guides. By repeating affirmations, you will strengthen your bond with the angels. Prayers will help you to communicate your own thoughts and feelings with them, while the blessings can be used to bring angelic bliss into your own life or that of somebody else. In some of the blessings, you will come across the term "living water," which refers to the constant flow of energy that courses through the universe—with which we can change the world and ourselves.

You may wish to write down some of the affirmations, prayers, and blessings so that you can carry them with you and draw on them whenever you want to. You will find many scattered throughout this book, but here are three to set you at your ease when you first try to draw angels to you:

an affirmation to help you to align with your angelic guides:

Each moment is a new beginning.
I use my angelic guides for perfect vision.

a prayer for protection:

Through the Beloved, I demand the angelic host's eternal protection.
May they come forth through me.

a blessing for yourself and others:

May the blessings of light be with you.
May this angelic presence illuminate your heart
and bring complete peace within.

If you practice these techniques daily, you will lay the stepping-stones that will help you to reach across to your angelic guides.

Good Luck!

We sincerely hope that reading this book will give you as much enjoyment as sharing our experiences and knowledge with you has given us. And we trust that you will continue to enjoy a wonderful journey of discovery with your own personal angel long after you have turned the last page. Your angel is forever yours.

angel
WISDOM

angels of guidance

As we will discover in this first chapter, angels are often there to help and guide us with, and also without, our knowledge of their involvement. They may provide help in the guise of an ordinary-looking person in modern dress; through arranging a series of coincidences that save the day; in the form of a voice, or even as a compulsion to act prompted by an inner intuitive angel. In whatever way these wonderful beings intervene, those involved are left in no doubt at all after the event that they have been truly guided by an angel.

THE VISIT

Emily arrived in the busy market town, her heart fluttering with anticipation. This was to be a very special day—she was meeting an old and dear friend for the first time in many years. Arriving at the clock tower where they had arranged to meet, Emily stared eagerly at the bustling crowd, searching impatiently for her friend. She was, however, quite early, and she began to recall all the days of fun they had shared as young girls. Now, both almost eighty, it was important to Emily that she meet Margaret one last time, before the terminal illness Emily was suffering from claimed her. She decided not to tell Margaret how ill she was, as that would mar the day and she wanted the last visit with her friend to be happy and joyful.

The minutes ticked away and soon an hour had passed. Emily began to worry and became very anxious, trying to decide what the reason might be for her friend being so late. It had been many years since they had visited this little market town, so perhaps she was lost; the town did actually look rather different. Perhaps her friend was unwell and had not been able to get in touch? By now Emily was feeling very tired and struggling to keep the tears at bay.

Suddenly in front of Emily, appeared a beautiful young lady who was smiling kindly and asking if she could help. Emily explained the situation, and the young lady merely nodded, saying, "Stay here one moment longer. I shall find your friend." Watching her go, Emily was struck by her beauty: she had the most delicate face, deep blue eyes, and very long blond hair. In what appeared to be the blinking of an eye, the lady returned, with Margaret beside her! Tears flowed as the friends hugged each other with relief. On turning to thank the young lady, they were astonished to find she had simply vanished. Mulling events over, they realized that Margaret had been waiting in the wrong place, but how on earth did the lady know who Margaret was? Emily had not given her a description, and of course she had no idea where Margaret might be in the bustling market. Finally they concluded that this was an angel of guidance, determined that they should meet one last time.

angel blessing

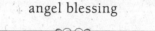

O heavenly angels, I open the gates of guidance and abundance.
My heart sings with living water and peace.
May this guidance bring complete love into my soul.

JOSH'S BIG ADVENTURE

The day had been such fun, Carol and Barbara had treated themselves to a shopping session in the city, having lunch, and enjoying being together. They did remark, laughingly, that age was creeping up on them because by midafternoon they definitely felt the need for refreshments and a good sit-down. Surprisingly, their favorite coffee shop was full as were several others. So they decided to return home and have coffee there. Driving along, Barbara suddenly exclaimed that she had forgotten to buy the one thing she really needed: some bread. They would have to take a diversion, through a nearby village to find a bakery. Calling her husband on her cell phone to ask if he needed anything from the village, Carol was surprised to find the phone would not work. She borrowed Barbara's and found that did not work either! It was very odd. Leaving the usual route home, they took the quiet road leading to the village. Carol suddenly froze. There, walking determinedly toward the busy main road, was her nine-year-old son, Josh. "Please stop," she yelled at Barbara. "I must get to him!"

Josh is no ordinary nine-year-old: he is autistic, and has no sense of danger at all. As he is never allowed outdoors alone, Carol could not believe that he was walking by himself so far from home. He was heading quickly toward the busy road. Seeing his mother, Josh started to run, thinking this a game of chase. He ran headlong across the road between the traffic, amazingly having pressed the button for a green light beforehand. This was a concept he had never been able to master previously. Eventually Carol breathlessly caught up with him, and gently took him back to the car. At home, Carol's husband—relieved to see Josh—explained what had happened. Early that afternoon, he had decided to take Josh out for an ice cream. However, just as he was about to start the car, he realized that his wallet was still indoors. Dashing into the house for only a few seconds, he was astonished to find on his return that Josh had left the car and was nowhere to be seen. He started to search but twenty frantic minutes later had called the police for help.

It was at this point, Carol started to take stock of the day's events. Josh had walked several miles away from home; he had passed a railway, crossing the bridge without trying to reach the trains, something he would always do because of his fascination with them. He had walked around a large, deep pond of water, another danger point, crossed many roads including an intersection filled with heavy traffic and no crossing point. It seemed a minor miracle. Then Carol mused on her day: if they had found a seat in the coffee shop, they would have been at least an hour later driving home, clearly missing Josh. Had they not taken a detour to the village, the same would have applied. Had the cell phones worked, they would have known that Josh was missing and driven straight home without going through the village, and once more missed Josh.

For some time Carol has thought that Josh has a guardian angel, so for her this was clear proof that he had been watched over and protected on his big adventure.

angel affirmations

I am open to my guardian angels.
I am protected and guided by my angels.
I trust that my guide will attract only miracles in my life.

WHEN ALL ELSE FAILS!

Everyone who has ever taken an examination can identify with Maria. Just before the big day, it feels as though your brain has reached the saturation point, and yet you feel the compulsion to continue studying. Maria lives in Moscow and wrote to tell me that she feels the angels are very close to her and that they guide her through life, perhaps never moreso than at the time of her most important examination in her computer studies course. The night before Maria's viva she was understandably nervous. This would be the final stage in a most important and necessary examination for her future career. She would have to give a lecture followed by questions. Midnight approached and Maria felt completely drained and exhausted. She had revised every aspect of her speech to the best of her ability, but she realized the questions could not be predicted and she dreaded questions in certain areas of her subject, knowing these to be weak points. Falling into bed with a feeling of despair, her thoughts were all on failure. Despite her anxiety, she was so tired that she was already half asleep as soon as her head hit the pillow.

In her dreamy state, she was suddenly aware of a strong sensation, a compulsion even, urging her to go to the computer once more and open her file. Her legs were so tired they would not move, and she had to summon every last ounce of energy to get out of bed. Telling herself that this was ridiculous, she switched on the computer and found the file. There was a strange, uncanny feeling that she was not moving her hand. It was as if another force had taken over. The file opened somewhere about halfway through, odd in itself, and Maria began to read the page on display. It was in fact a section she had not thought particularly important and had spent little time revising. Closing the computer down she returned to bed, thinking how silly she had been.

Her speech went well and the examiners proceeded to the questions they felt needed a full answer. To Maria's astonishment the first question was about the exact section she had read so late the previous night. She could recall details with complete clarity, and answered so fully that she feels this was the deciding factor in her success. To this day, she firmly believes the angels guided her hand that night and helped her through the examination.

We all have free will and can ignore our inner voice if we so choose. Maria certainly could have done so and would never have known how her angel helped her. Before moving on to our first exercise in this chapter, let us contemplate the following wise words:

> I believe that we are free within limits, and yet there is an unseen hand, a guiding angel, that somehow like a submerged propeller, drives us on.
>
> RABINDRANATH TAGORE

angel meditation

Sit or lie comfortably in a dark area. Visualize yourself surrounded by a cloud of white light energy. Open your mind and heart, and let in your guardian angel. When your guardian angel comes, whether as an image or a special feeling, call to it and embrace it.

Open your heart, and let the angelic vibration enter your whole body. Speak to your angel, and let the energy shift your thoughts or feelings.

Repeat silently throughout your meditation:

My heart sings with love for my Angel of Guidance.

Let the angelic energy take over your being. When you feel ready, thank your guide and let yourself surface to the outer consciousness.

ANGEL IN THE STORM

It had been a very long week, John thought as he drove home. After many hours spent working and even more driving, he longed to be back with his wife and children. But driving conditions were atrocious, with the heavy rain making progress difficult and thunder and lightning now adding to the problem. Spurred on by the fact that he only had a few miles to go, John tried to hurry against the odds. Approaching the fork in the road, which indicated only a couple of miles left to cover, he was shaken by a huge clap of thunder and an enormous zigzag of lightning just ahead. Slowing down, he approached the fork in the road, only to discover to his dismay that a huge tree had been felled by the lightning and was lying right across his path. He shouted out in sheer frustration; no way could he pass this obstacle, and it meant he would have to take the other fork. This involved driving the long way round to reach home, which would add a further five miles or so to his journey.

At last the lights of home shone through the trees: he was safe and enormously relieved to be with his family. Relating the problem of the fallen tree to his wife, he smiled when she replied, "I think the angels protected you. After all a few more yards along the road and the tree might have fallen on top of you." She did have a point, he conceded. Perhaps it had been a fortunate escape.

The following morning, the village was full of stories about damage to property, but the big talking point, however, was about the road leading from the village. Workmen were building a barrier preventing anyone driving along this stretch of road. It appeared that during the previous night's storm, the road had simply collapsed, leaving a huge, water-filled hole in the middle. The road would be out of use until extensive repairs had been made. John felt a shiver go up his spine. Had the tree not prevented him from driving down that road, he would surely have driven straight into the gaping hole, and who knows what the consequences of that would have been. His wife gave him a hug.

"Now do you believe in angels?" she asked.

"I certainly do!" John replied.

Let your light shine as a beacon, guiding home the traveler with the light of love.

WILLIAM SWINFIELD THAW

angel prayer

May the angels guide me with divine love.
I know divine guidance watches over me and creates a
   clear path.
I am now reborn spiritually, bringing divine love, light,
   and truth into all my experiences.

The Inner Angel

After the hustle and bustle of the big city, it is always a pleasure for Connie and David to take their family for a long stay in their summer seaside home. Philadelphia disappears into the distance and the prospect of a quiet and peaceful stay lies ahead. One morning, shortly after their arrival, the sound of tree felling and of grinding machines dealing with the tree stumps shattered the air of tranquillity. Connie and David were trying to chat on the front porch while the noise surrounded them. Without any particular motive, Connie suddenly stood up and walked to the backyard, confusing her husband, who was midsentence. It was unlike Connie to simply get up and leave when he was talking to her. David thought it very odd behavior indeed.

Arriving at the back of the house, Connie found to her horror that Barbara, their next-door neighbor, was facedown in her garden pond. In a flash, Connie realized what had happened. It had been a sad and difficult year for Barbara since losing her husband. Missing him dreadfully, she had felt depressed and lonely, sleeping fitfully and losing her appetite. She was at this point very thin and frail. Connie realized that Barbara was struggling to gain a foot- or handhold on the bottom of the pond, but she was completely without the strength to do so. Connie knew that she was in serious trouble and shouted for her husband to come and help her. However, it was simply impossible for him to hear her, as the noise from the tree cutting was too great. Grasping Barbara under her arms,

Connie pulled with all her might and managed to haul her onto the side of the pond.

It took a while, but Barbara eventually stopped coughing and shaking, becoming calm and able to relate events to Connie. It appeared that she had slipped, falling into the pond, which was not terribly deep, but the bottom was covered in algae and she could not get a grip with her hands or feet. She was so weak, she could not lift her face above the water and was clearly about to drown.

"How did you know I was in trouble?" Barbara asked, and Connie could not think of an answer. The fact was that she had felt some inner force make her rise from the chair, as if in a dream, and walk to her neighbor's backyard. David says how very strange it was to see Connie walk away in such a manner. Goose bumps break out on Connie when she thinks about the incident and how close Barbara came to drowning that morning. She told Barbara it was a sure sign that God loved her and had guided Connie's inner angel to Barbara's aid in such a time of danger.

I shall walk where nature leads me,
I shall place my trust in a higher power,
I shall return guarded and guided by love.

ANON

If, as Connie did, we listen to the inner voice and trust the love we have for others in our hearts, we too will be guided by our angel-led instincts in life.

guiding light insight

Your Guardian Angel will never order you to do anything. Your angel will only suggest or offer the information to you. This will only enter through a sign, feeling, or light energy around you.

To invoke your angel of guidance, repeat three times:

Guardian Angel of Guidance, come to me.
I call upon my guide for complete protection.

JANE'S ANGEL

It had been a long hot day and Jane felt completely drained of energy. Her job was proving to be very stressful, even though she was usually happy with her legal career. Every evening for the past two weeks, Jane had visited the hospice on her way home from work to spend some time with her much-loved grandmother. All her life, Jane had been close to her grandmother and adored her. The feeling was mutual and the old lady perked up dramatically as soon as Jane arrived. Time was running out, however, and all the family understood that

Grandmother's remaining time with them would be quite short. That particular evening, even though Jane's arrival brought a cheerful smile to her face, Jane thought her grandmother was looking especially frail. Leaving for home Jane felt tearful, though she cheered up slightly to see her parents arriving as she drove away.

It was bliss to be home and, after a quick snack, Jane took a drink into the garden to sit and relax. Her life had truly been blessed, she thought, growing up in a happy home with a wonderful supportive grandmother, and now having a successful career that enabled Jane to have her own lovely little house and independence. The light was beginning to fade and Jane considered going indoors to get an early night in preparation for another busy day. Suddenly, only a few yards away from Jane in the garden, a light appeared, growing in intensity as she watched, transfixed. To her disbelief, in the middle of this bright light appeared a full-blown angel! Jane literally rubbed her eyes, unable to comprehend what she was witnessing. The angel grew clearer if anything, and Jane could distinguish the features, which on reflection she felt were quite androgynous. No words, music, or sounds of any kind accompanied this vision, and gradually the angel began to simply fade away. Jumping to her feet, as if waking, Jane realized exactly what this must mean: Grandmother needed her. Seizing her car keys, she fled to her parked car and drove to the hospice.

In the entrance hall, her mother was just about to use the telephone. Heaving a sigh of relief when Jane hurried into the hall, she said, "I was just about to call you—Grandma is fading, and we knew you would want to be here."

Rushing to Grandmother's room, Jane sat beside her and held her hand. The old lady gave it a squeeze without opening her eyes. "It's me, Grandma," said Jane. Another squeeze—she knew her much-loved granddaughter was with her. Within minutes Grandmother had slipped away to the next life. It was only much later that night, the full implication of what had happened in the garden hit Jane. She had been summoned by an angel to be with her grandmother in her final moments. "What a privilege and a blessing," she said out loud, "to have had such an experience." Jane knew she would remember it all her life.

Angels are there to guide us throughout our lives. We may not all receive such obvious guidance as the people in this chapter, but the guidance is there all the same. We must be open to the signs, which are often very subtle, but if we truly believe, the angels will make their presence felt and their guidance clear.

angel blessing

May a blessed light shine upon you,
surround you, and protect you.

~ 2 ~

angels of healing

here are many stories about angels who have brought healing to people caught in a crisis or troubled by a health issue. Angels can teach us to work with them as healers, and as spiritual guides. As you begin to trust your angels, you can take the next step to access their healing powers. This simply means asking them for their guidance and help.

Although many of you will be able to see results with your angels clearly, we will cover an exercise that you will have to practice until it becomes a familiar task—almost a routine. The secret to making a connection with an angel is: don't give up! Your reasoning mind will start to work in harmony with the spiritual side of your brain. Once you achieve your angel connection and have a fixed purpose you will start to see results, so be persistent.

When life presents us with a crisis, many of us may become so low that we open ourselves up automatically to divine

17

intervention. The very reason that our spiritual banks are completely empty, and we feel totally drained, makes us open to receive help. At this very moment, the angels can come to us, just as they did for Edna in the following story.

HEARTBREAK

It is not unusual for someone to have an amazing angelic experience and keep the fact to themselves for many years. There are many reasons why this is so, not the least being the fear that people will laugh or the belief that it was so powerful an event they feel it was only for them to savor and not share with others. Whatever the reason was, Edna decided to keep her story private, and it was only many years after the event itself that she decided to share it with her sister Gaye.

Losing a loved one in death is terrible, but when someone you love leaves you for another in this life it is also a kind of bereavement. When her husband went to be with someone else, Edna was left to take care of a son who was just two years of age. Quite apart from her emotional turmoil there were practical worries also. It was the most awful time and Edna was in great distress.

Home was a large Victorian house in London, separated into three apartments. Edna lived in the one on the ground floor. One morning, standing at the bedroom window, gazing out in sheer misery, Edna broke down into tears. Sobbing uncontrollably, she despaired as to how on earth she would cope. Suddenly through the tears, Edna became aware of a figure taking shape outside her bedroom window, so clear and bright that it is as distinct in her mind today as it was on that morning. She stared in disbelief at an angel, wings half folded as it stood perfectly still gazing directly at her. Feelings of peace and calm swept over her, and she felt surrounded by love. Surely, things would work out in her life now, she reasoned. The experience was so amazing that it gave her strength and a feeling of being loved, enabling her to carry on.

It was not easy at first: two years of struggle followed but Edna was sustained by a firm frame of mind, and the knowledge that she was cared for. It was then that she met her second husband. He is a wonderful partner, and with him came three more children to complete her family. Edna had found the happiness that she longed for and that she continues to enjoy to this very day.

Saying Good-bye

Healing an aching heart, as we have seen, is just one of the ways in which angels influence our lives. Their method of healing is always appropriate to our needs. Saskia has a moving story to tell about the loss of her mother and how the angels were able to help heal her heavy heart.

Scotland had always attracted Saskia and her family. Perhaps, as Dutch people living in Holland, they were attracted to the mountains because of the contrast with their homeland. It was during a lovely May when Saskia, her husband, and parents left for a two-week holiday in Scotland. Sadly, Saskia's mother soon became unwell, developing a persistent cough. As soon as the family returned to Holland, Saskia's mother sought medical advice. It was a dreadful shock to all the family to learn after investigation that the problem was due to lung cancer. It appeared that the cancer was so invasive that there was little hope. Radiation treatment was begun, but only a few short months after the holiday, Saskia's mother died.

The day of her mother's death was all the more painful for Saskia as her mother slipped into a coma rapidly before she could say good-bye to her. Desperately wanting to tell her mother how much she was loved, Saskia felt her grief was deepened by the fact that this had not been possible. It was a dreadful shock to all the family to see her slip away without warning.

Two days after her mother's death, Saskia woke early in the morning. It would be two more days until the funeral, and this was a very difficult week indeed. Sitting upright in bed, Saskia became aware of a strong, pervasive scent of flowers. She thought it was a mixture of jasmine and lilies maybe, but whatever it was, the whole bedroom was filled with this wonderful fragrance. There were no flowers in the room, and yet when Saskia's husband woke he too could smell the powerful perfume. After a few moments the fragrance began to fade, and Saskia felt a strong feeling of comfort. Instinctively she knew that this was her mother in the angelic realms saying good-bye to her daughter in a gentle and loving way. Saskia says that she felt her mother was conveying to her that she was safe in heaven. The experience is as clear, comforting, and powerful today as on that special morning.

Angels work with us in whatever way they can to help us heal our lives. Not usually by doing the work for us, but by showing us what we need to do and supporting us with extra love, wisdom, encouragement, and peace.

EILEEN ELIAS FREEMAN

angel blessing

O heavenly angels, I open the gates of healing and sincerity.
My heart sings with living water and peace.
May this healing bring complete love into my soul.

COMFORT FOR CHILDREN

Our next angel stories feature angels comforting children in times of illness or fear. The first story concerns a little girl who suffered dreadfully from chest infections. Each winter, bouts of infection would recur frequently, making Brenda's life a misery. Today, as an adult looking back, she realizes just how debilitating these bouts of illness were. It was common practice when Brenda was a child to treat chest infections with a steam kettle. This would humidify the air, facilitating an easier flow of air to the lungs. Brenda's mother and father would carry her bed downstairs and in effect make a steam room for her.

One night, when feeling particularly poorly, Brenda woke to find the room flooded in a warm glow. She felt no fear or distress but simply watched in wonder as a figure emerged at the foot of her bed. It was fairly small in stature, and radiated a pale light. She knew immediately that this was an angel. The family all attended church and believed in God and his angels, enabling Brenda to accept this vision completely.

The following morning, Brenda's mother was amazed at how much improved her daughter was—it felt like a minor miracle. The memory of that night is treasured and, as is the case with so many children who experience an angel when young, it has remained crystal clear for Brenda to this day. It is also interesting to note that the angel described by Brenda was "small in stature"; this is a description I hear frequently and I am convinced that angels appear smaller to children in order not to alarm them. We always receive what we are able to cope with. Children believe in angels, they are close to them and trust in their healing help instinctively. To receive healing for ourselves, we must become as open as little children.

Children always believe in angels. It's mutual.

KAREN GOLDMAN

angel meditation

Sit or lie comfortably in a dark area. Visualize yourself surrounded by a cloud of green light energy. Open your mind and heart and let your guardian angel in. When your guardian angel enters, let the vibration fill your whole body.

Repeat silently through your meditation:

My heart sings with love for my Angel of Healing.

Let the angelic energy take over your being. When you feel ready, thank your guide and let yourself gradually surface to the outer consciousness.

divine key

Talk with your angel. Be specific with your healing needs. You can ask for healing for a loved one, healing for a health problem or a situation, or direct healing light to be sent to a specific part of your body. Remember, the more you ask, the more you will receive.

FEAR OF THE UNKNOWN

To Wendy, a trip to Scotland sounded wonderful; it would almost be like going to a foreign country, even though the Scottish border was only forty miles away from her home. The whole family had been invited to stay with friends who lived in a large stone house in the most beautiful countryside. Wendy would be visiting these friends of her parents for the first time, and they in turn were looking forward to meeting her. Several animals, including goats and pigs, were kept in the garden of this old house. It will be wonderful, thought Wendy. The best thing of all, however, for Wendy as an only child, was the thought of several children virtually the same age as her to play with. The twins, Martin and Malcolm, were a year older at eight and Sarah just six months younger—it was going to be such fun!

The first sight of the house in Scotland took their breath away: it was huge, built of gray stone, and surrounded by wonderful woods. Wendy thought it looked rather like a castle, and her mother and father agreed. It had been many years since Wendy's parents and their friends had been together and they were all so happy to meet again. Initially the children were all shy and quite wary of each other, and, if truth be told, Wendy had a little trouble understanding the broad Scottish accent. By the second day, however, they were all good friends and having a lovely time playing together. There seemed to be space everywhere, inside and outside the house; it was a wonderful sense of freedom for Wendy. One day they woke to a dreadful thunderstorm, and it was clear that they would have to play indoors that day. Martin suggested a game of hide-and-seek, which everyone thought was a splendid idea. It was great fun, with so many wonderful hiding places in the house. Warming to the game, Wendy suddenly had a great idea. Slowly pushing open the door to the cellar she tiptoed inside and crept down the stone steps feeling sure they would not think of looking for her there.

Time passed slowly and soon Wendy began to feel cold and slightly fearful. It was in fact quite dark in the cellar, so she decided to give in and climb the steep steps out. On reaching the heavy wooden door at the top of the cellar steps, Wendy discovered that she could not open it, it must have locked behind her when she had entered. Panic gripped her and she began to bang on the door and cry out loud for help. No one came. The house was so big, plus the fact that the children and adults were two stories above the cellar meant they could not hear her. Shaking and sobbing Wendy was by now on the verge of panic. What on earth could she do? At this point she suddenly started to feel a warmth envelop her, and she stopped shaking. There was a strong sensation of arms around her, and she felt at once calm and loved. She had stopped crying, and although she felt a huge relief on hearing steps above her head, she had lost all fear.

The cellar door swung open and her mother's face appeared. Cradling her daughter in her arms, her mother explained that the heavy door had indeed locked behind her, and that it took a while for everyone to realize that she was missing. Each and every child and adult hugged and kissed her, making Wendy feel wonderful and cherished. They remarked on how brave she was, not even succumbing to tears!

Wendy kept her secret until she was alone that night with her mother. Tucking her daughter up in bed that night, Wendy's mother listened attentively to her little girl's account of events. At last she said, "I think you had your own guardian angel looking after you today darling," and Wendy knew this was the correct explanation. Several times over the years, Wendy has experienced the same warm feeling of arms around her in times of fear. She has never doubted that this is her own special angel.

guiding light insight

You can bring the angels closer to you through invocations and prayer.

To invoke your healing angel, repeat three times:

Guardian Angel of Healing, come to me.
I call upon my guide for complete protection.

FEAR OF THE DARK

Wan is a Chinese lady who is married to an Englishman and lives in London. Growing up in Hong Kong, she attended a university in the city before finally leaving to take up postgraduate study in London. Her story, however, takes place when she was a child in Hong Kong. In keeping with all childhood experiences, the memory remains as clear today as it did in far-off Hong Kong in her early days.

Hong Kong was still occupied by the Japanese army in those days, and Wan says one of her vivid memories is of the darkness covering the city after nightfall. There were no streetlamps, and this made the bedrooms extremely dark, frightening Wan. One of her female relatives shared her bedroom, giving her a little more confidence. The apartment occupied by the family was very large, with high ceilings, and at the end of Wan's bed was a tall window overlooking a yard.

All appeared normal one winter evening when Wan crept into her bed. Suddenly, however, in the middle of the night, Wan realized that she was alone. Having stretched out her hand to touch her aunt in the next bed, she was horrified to find it empty. She was totally alone—the darkness appeared deeper than ever in her state of terror. Sobbing, she screamed out in fright, closing her eyes tight against the dark. Opening her eyes gingerly, she was transfixed to see a figure by the tall window at the foot of her bed. It took a while to register that this was in fact an angel. Wan's angel was indeed huge, as tall as the window and glowing with what she describes as an almost green hue. How clearly she saw it in the gloom and how wonderful was the feeling of love and protection. The angel had enormous stationary wings composed of delicate feathers. No movement of any kind took place, but the angel's presence alleviated Wan's fear, which subsided immediately. This little girl was so terrified that it required a huge angel to calm her, rare among children.

The saddest part of this story is the fact that Wan felt loved for the very first time. She says her parents did not show her love and the feeling was completely alien to her. This fact dramatically intensified the experience. Feelings of comfort, warmth, and protection washed over her; it was indeed quite wonderful. Slowly the angel started to fade and Wan felt sad to see it leave. She closed her eyes tight and reopened them several times quite forcefully, in the hope that this would bring her angel back. The angel had indeed gone, she realized, and eventually she fell into a deep, peaceful sleep. The angel had left behind such amazing love that to this day Wan says whenever she thinks of that night, those feelings of love and warmth return. The closing comment about her story comes from Wan: she says her guardian angel has guided and protected her all through life and "such," she says "is the love of God."

Angels are with us for life. So many people speak of experiences of an angelic nature that occurred when they were young and feel certain for the rest of their lives that the angel is ever near them. It is as if once the bridge between heaven and humans has been crossed, the angels use it to visit us forever. Be open to this prospect as you repeat the following affirmations to yourself.

angel affirmations

I am open to my healing angels.
I am always healthy, whole, and complete.
I allow my Inner Light to shine bright.

divine key

We are each a living bridge, sharing our gifts and making a difference in this world. When we open up and become a bridge to the world, it is up to each of us to move, touch, and inspire others. We must cross over into the world of transformation as a way of being. By calling on the angels of healing we can empower ourselves and others to live up to this vision. We must all help to create a world that works for everyone.

HEALING THE SOUL

In England it is the role of doctors to administer the MMR injection to babies who are around twelve months old. This is a recommended procedure to protect children from the childhood diseases of mumps, measles, and rubella. It is a triple vaccine that has caused a great deal of controversy among the medical profession and parents. In some cases the injection has allegedly been linked to the onset of autism, a frightening thought to contemplate, although the evidence is inconclusive. Many worried parents have opted not to let their babies have the injection at all. Such action is frowned upon by the authorities, owing to the fact that these childhood diseases can be very serious and are once more becoming prominent in certain areas. Other parents have paid a great deal of money to let their child have three separate injections, believing this to be far safer and with no apparent risk involved. However, in the face of all this controversy, the majority of doctors and the Health Service insist that there is no proven connection between the injection and the condition of autism.

In light of all this, you can imagine Melissa's inner turmoil when the time came for her little daughter to have the injection. Alternately, waves of confidence and fear washed over Melissa, and despite long debates with her husband, she felt bewildered as to what she should do. Eventually it was decided that their little girl should have the vaccine, and Melissa tried to stay calm. At this point, Melissa read a magazine article advising people to ask the angels for help in times of trouble. Believing in angels, Melissa thought this was sound advice and asked the angels for guidance. The night before the treatment, Melissa was pottering around the house completing minor chores while her husband bathed their little girl. Suddenly, overwhelmed by powerful sensations of calmness, reassurance, and contentment, she knew that they had made the right decision and this was the angels' answer.

The following morning, Melissa fully expected her fear to return but she was still imbued with calm and confidence wrapped around her like a protective cloak. Her little daughter suffered no ill effects whatsoever, and her mother thanks the angels for getting her through such a difficult time.

angel blessing

May blessings of eternal loving-kindness
Radiate around you and throughout the world.

angel prayer

May the Angels guide my life.
In every ray of light that shines,
In every drop of rain,
Angels are present.
I am a perfect spirit, speaking perfect words.

❧ 3 ❧

angels of wisdom

ost of us are aware that knowledge comes from books, teachings, and life experiences. We start learning the minute we choose to arrive in our souls on this earth, and we enter this life with a blueprint of how we are to fulfill our lessons. True wisdom comes from the Inner Source, your internal angel, which can be accessed through the angelic exercises in these pages.

Angelic help is infinite and unlimited. Just ask. But you must act quickly on the guidance and wisdom you receive. The more you exercise your angelic qualities the more you will witness these qualities in others. We can all be incidental angels with a little practice. Children often understand this concept automatically and with refreshing simplicity, and our first story illustrates this fact beautifully.

A MINOR MIRACLE

Lily is as beautiful as her name and much loved. One bright sunny morning in Chapel, Lily was sitting on her mother's knee listening to the minister. The minister, Rev. Beryl Allerton of Stand Unitarian Chapel, had chosen a favorite poem of hers by the American Walt Whitman. The poem is inspiring verse about everyday miracles. Beryl continued to talk about miracles, including the very special miracle of a small child climbing onto one's lap and giving you a hug. At this point, Lily, who was only eighteen months old, scrambled down from her mother's lap and walked in a very determined fashion down the aisle of the chapel. Halting at one particular pew, she climbed onto the lap of a lady sitting there, threw her arms around her neck, and gave the lady a hug. The entire congregation gasped, and many shed a tear, as they realized Lily had chosen to hug a lady called Jessie, who was recently bereaved and saddened at the loss of her husband after a lifetime together. Snuggling down onto Jessie's lap, Lily remained there for the rest of the service.

Lily was indeed a miracle, and truly an angel of wisdom.

A miracle is never lost. It may touch many people you have not even met, and produce undreamed of changes in situations of which you are not even aware.

FROM *A COURSE IN MIRACLES*

OUT OF THE MOUTHS OF BABES

A few years ago I (Glennyce) accepted an invitation to speak in a large bookstore about angels. I was to read stories from my books and talk in general about angels in our lives today. A fairly large crowd assembled, eagerly awaiting pearls of wisdom! My attention was drawn to a small child of about four years old, sitting on her father's lap. A little girl of exquisite beauty, she sat transfixed the whole time I was speaking. I was astonished to see that she neither wriggled nor spoke, appearing to understand everything I was saying. At the end of my talk, people formed a queue in order for me to sign copies of my books for them. Glancing up, I saw the little girl and her father leaving and felt a great sadness as I wished to speak to her.

Eventually, the crowd thinned, and I was thrilled to see the little girl appear once more holding her father's hand. "We would like to buy the book *Children and Angels* please," he said, "and my daughter would love you to sign it." With great pleasure I signed the book and bending down, handed it to the little girl. Before I could speak, she gave the book to her daddy, and promptly threw her arms around my neck.

Whispering in my ear she told me, "You know I have an angel don't you; all little boys and girls do!" I was taken aback by the expressive and knowing look she then gave me.

"Yes," I whispered back. "Thank you for telling me." Her daddy smiled indulgently, and I wondered if he realized just how special his little daughter was. A friend witnessing the scene asked what the child had said, and when I told her she replied, "I rather think she herself was the angel." There was such a powerful feeling of a presence in the room, I could only agree.

angel blessing

❦

O heavenly angels, I open the gates of wisdom and knowledge.
My heart sings with living water and peace.
May this wisdom bring complete love into my soul.

CHERUBS

There can be few people, no matter how convinced they are that angels exist, who do not have moments of doubt. Deb was no exception, finding herself at one point pondering the subject and vacillating between incredulity and certainty. For some time she had been fascinated by the concept of angels and had started to read books about them.

One evening she had been studying intently the angel information in a particular book. Having completed a chapter that documented angel hierarchy and the myriad ways in which angels would help if asked, she found herself feeling greatly confused. It was a new concept for her, asking angels to help, even though she did believe in their existence most of the time. Deb longed for clarification, and, unsure of how this would come about, decided to ask God—after all, He was the font of all wisdom! She simply asked out loud to be shown that the information she had just acquired was in fact true. Pondering this for a moment she added that maybe a dream would be her chosen medium, a gentle way to see an angel.

Falling into a deep sleep, she does not recall dreaming anything at all. However, suddenly a loud voice urged her to wake, saying that there was someone who wished to see her. The voice was most insistent and, as Deb woke, she became fully aware that she was not alone. Sitting upright in bed, she could make out the outline of a figure in the half-light and she recalls thinking that she was decidedly unimpressed! Could this really be an angel? No light or warmth appeared to emanate from the figure and, as it faded, Deb lay down again on her pillow. It was at this moment she had the surprise of her life, for resting on the pillow was not one but two cherubs! They were of purest white and radiating love and light, not of this world, she says. She felt ecstatic, as if nothing else in the world was of any consequence. After only a couple of minutes, the cherubs faded and Deb was once more alone. This time, however, there was no uncertainty—all her doubts had been addressed. She told me that she was indeed the happiest person in the universe and fell into a deep untroubled sleep.

For days after the event, Deb wandered around in a state of awe and wonder, unsure what to do next. Eventually, she decided to look up the meaning of cherubs and was surprised to find that they signified wisdom. To this day, several years later, Deb asks herself why she was so privileged to have her prayer answered so promptly and to receive such a visit. She does know, however, that after her angelic encounter she took a long hard look at her life and made several changes that resulted in a happier, more peaceful way of life.

HOMEWARD BOUND

The multistory parking lot was deserted as Elizabeth hurried to reach her car. It had been a wonderful evening, for she loved trips to the theater and this had been an excellent play. Afterward, she had enjoyed a lovely meal along with her friends in a city center restaurant, and now, although very happy, she felt quite tired. Recalling she would have to be at work early the following day, she rushed to reach her car, eager to be on her way home. Glancing around she was aware that there were only a few cars still parked in this huge lot and that it was rather late and quite dark. A shiver of fear ran down her spine as she struggled to find her keys in the bottom of her handbag. Her fears were actually justified, for looming in front of the car suddenly, was a large menacing figure, arm raised as if to strike Elizabeth.

The full implication of what was about to befall her dawned on Elizabeth and in a second she found herself saying silently, "Angels please help me!" The man instantly appeared to freeze with his hand above his head, while staring intently at the passenger side of the car. "Sorry, governor," he said. "Didn't see you there," and, turning on his heel, he fled. Elizabeth looked toward the other side of the car, behind the car, and indeed walked all around the car—she was totally alone! There was no one else on the entire parking lot floor. She was completely bewildered. What could have happened, she mused.

Starting the car, it suddenly hit her: of course, she had asked the angels to help and they had answered her. The man clearly saw someone else by her car; a man he assumed to be her companion but visible only to him. How truly wise the angels are, she thought, and said a little prayer to thank them for their help in such a frightening situation.

SHADOWS AND WINGS

Gary and I are always delighted when a letter pops through the door with an exotic stamp on the envelope. It is wonderful reading the stories from people all around the world. It is confirmation, if indeed that were needed, of how the angels help globally with such wisdom and insight. Isabel wrote from her home in Timaru, New Zealand, but her amazing experience happened in Singapore. Visiting her son and family, Isabel was having a lovely time and enjoying all the new culture Singapore had to offer. It was decided that Isabel and her son's mother-in-law would take a trip together and explore the Indian quarter of the city. The sights, sounds, fragrances, and wonderful colors of this area were a delight, and both ladies enjoyed the experience very much. If there was a downside to this outing it was the heat, and after several hours exploring, Isabel began to feel that they should find a taxi to take them home.

It was at this point, while looking for a taxi that Isabel realized that they were in fact walking in the wrong direction along a one-way street. Turning down a side street they expected to reach the parallel road in the hope that a taxi would appear, enabling them to be quickly on their way home. Moving away from the main street appeared to bring more than a few worries, as the buildings were old and almost derelict. They experienced a feeling of menace. They had obviously strayed into one of those less desirable areas that are common to all big cities and that are best avoided. The two ladies thought it wise to walk in the middle of the road, but the sun beat down fiercely and Isabel felt decidedly unhappy and very vulnerable. Her companion was a small, frail lady, and Isabel shuddered to think what would happen next. Fear and heat gripped Isabel as the reality of their situation dawned.

Inexplicably, a large shadow suddenly fell over Isabel and her companion. It covered them with shade as though symbolically protecting them from harm. The shadow remained overhead, forming an island of protection, as they walked the entire length of the road. There was simply no explanation as to the source of this welcome help. At last they reached the end of the road, where mercifully they saw a taxi pull up for them. Sinking into their seats they were overwhelmed with relief. Surprisingly, says Isabel, it was some time later that the truth hit her and she suddenly knew exactly what had happened. She told me Psalm 91 came into her head. Looking this up in the Bible, I found the following: "We live within the shadow of the Almighty." The fourth verse states: "He will shield you with his wings." Isabel has little doubt that she had been beneath angel wings, sent by God that day to protect them in Singapore.

angel meditation

Sit or lie comfortably in a darkened room. Visualize a cloud of blue light energy surrounding you. Open your mind and heart, and welcome your guardian angel of wisdom. When your guardian angel comes to you, let the vibration fill your body and mind.

Repeat silently through your meditation:

My heart sings with love for my Angel of Wisdom.

Let the angelic energy take over your being. When you are ready, thank your guide and let yourself surface to outer consciousness.

A HELPING HAND

Losing someone we love is often the most difficult event we will ever have to face in our lives. To cope with the loss of a son or daughter is especially distressing for the parent. So many times I have heard the expression that this is "against the natural order." Gaye told me this inspiring story about her daughter, Heather, which she sincerely hopes may comfort others in similar circumstances.

Heather lived alone and, one bright sunny morning, she woke to find herself in a most unusual position. One arm was raised above her head and resting on the pillow. She could not recall ever having woken in such a position before, and it did seem rather odd. She was then aware of an amazing sensation: someone was actually holding her hand!

Keeping perfectly still, Heather allowed her eyes to roam around the room, simply to convince herself that she was in fact awake and not dreaming. She remained in that position, totally and completely unafraid, with the wonderful feeling of a firm hand in hers. The minute she moved, however, the sensation disappeared. It had been simply amazing—strong, solid, and very real, a definite hand holding hers. Sharing this experience with her mother, she told Gaye how fantastic it had felt, and Gaye was happy for her daughter, agreeing that it must indeed have been wonderful.

Sadly, some time later, Heather was diagnosed with cancer and, much to everyone's distress, died. How prophetic and symbolic does that morning's experience now seem. To have an angel hold one's hand before such a diagnosis is truly remarkable. How lovely it would be to think that her angel was there to hold her hand when she left this world. Gaye says that she often feels her presence. Although she would dearly love a sign also confirming this, she is comforted by the fact that her beloved daughter was visited in such a heartwarming and wise way.

Because we may not have witnessed an angel with our own eyes, it does not mean they are not there. They leave signs and clues everywhere, but we just do not recognize them. Often the only way of perceiving an angel is by the lovely glow left behind when they are gone. Try the following exercise and keep an open mind.

guiding light insight

Trust and hand everything over to your angels during the time of invocation. Angels work with everyone regardless of personal histories and beliefs. Release all expectations of how your request will be manifested and they will respond to your unconditional love.

To invoke your angel of wisdom, repeat three times:

Guardian Angel of Wisdom, come to me,
I call upon my guide for complete wisdom.

No Smoke Without Angels?

People often tell me that an angelic experience happened to them at one point in their lives, and not only have they never forgotten it, but, indeed, they wish they could have another such wonderful encounter. Occasionally, I meet someone for whom angels seem to be ever close, and many experiences happen throughout their lives. Connie is one such person. I first met this lovely lady when her son, Kyle, was seriously ill and I included her amazing story of angelic intervention in my book *Angels and Miracles*. In an earlier chapter in this book, we read how Connie was moved by the angels to help a neighbor. It would appear that Connie is very open to the angelic realm and that they are ever mindful of her circumstances. The story of Connie's trip to the seaside clearly illustrates this point.

Connie's father was an excellent mechanic. He owned a garage and there was little he did not know about cars and how to fix them. When it came to looking after family vehicles, you can imagine just how thorough he was and how safe his family felt. One day, Connie decided that it would be nice to take her children, Krystle (aged three) and Kyle (just one year old) to the seashore. They had never seen the sea, and Connie and her husband thought it would be fun to introduce them to a few amusement rides at the same time. The children being tiny, they both had to have a car seat and, as everyone who has ever taken small children for a ride will know, they needed many other additional items. It was decided to take Connie's father up on his offer to drive his larger car, an Oldsmobile, which would afford them more space and comfort than the one they owned.

All was packed into the car for the day trip to New Jersey, and in good spirits they waved good-bye. They traveled across the Tacony Bridge, connecting Pennsylvania with New Jersey, driving on the main highway. All of a sudden, for no apparent reason the car began to produce copious amounts of smoke from the engine. Connie and her husband were totally baffled, knowing that her dad had recently fine-tuned the car, which was always in perfect condition anyway. Soon the smoke was so dense that they could not see out of the car windows and, spotting a garage, they thankfully pulled in. The mechanic rushed out, astonished to see so much smoke pouring from the engine. He opened the hood and checked the water. It was full, so he proceeded to check everything else he could possibly think of. But nothing untoward could be found. At this point, everyone was totally perplexed. Connie said, "I shall call my dad and see if he has any ideas." To say Connie's dad was surprised would be an understatement: "That car was in perfect running order!" he said. "I made sure of it." He was totally puzzled when his daughter told him that the smoke was in fact so thick that they simply could not continue to drive.

Replacing the receiver, Connie turned to leave the phone booth and walk back to her family, when suddenly a lady came rushing into the garage in a dreadful state. "Please," she shouted, "give me the phone! There has been a dreadful multi-car accident. We need ambulances; many people have been hurt." Swiftly jumping out of the way, Connie left the phone booth. She and her family watched transfixed as the ambulances arrived on the scene with great speed.

It finally dawned on Connie that, had they not pulled into the garage, they too would have been in the middle of this awful accident. Eventually the children were placed back into the car and they set off, anxious to return home now that the smoke had stopped. For the entire return journey, the car behaved perfectly, no trace of smoke at any point.

Arriving home, Connie's father inspected the car with great care. There was nothing at all wrong and no reason whatsoever for the engine to have produced smoke. It had never happened previously, and the following day Connie's father continued to drive the car without incident, as indeed he did for a long time after that experience.

Both Connie and Dave, her husband, firmly believe in guardian angels and are convinced that both their mothers guard them from heaven. The smoke had forced them to stop out of harm's way—of that they have no doubt.

angel affirmations

I choose to say yes to success in all areas of my life.
I let the inner wisdom of truth shine in my life.
My life is a magnificent blessing of peace and trust.

A Very Difficult Day

It had simply been one of those days. The more Louise tried to hurry, the less she appeared to achieve. It was now midafternoon, and here she was running late for the children's dental appointments while desperately trying to get her elderly aunt off the telephone. Finally she interrupted, "I am going to end this conversation, Aunt Barbara. I really have to go," and quickly replaced the receiver. Luke and Amy found themselves manhandled into their coats, and quickly they all climbed into the car. "No, no, no!" Louise yelled, as the car refused to start. It was quite impossible, she thought. The car had been working normally all day as she had already been in and out of the house on many journeys and experienced no problems; in fact, this was the most reliable car she had ever driven. But no amount of revving or peering under the hood made a scrap of difference: it simply would not start.

Reaching into her coat pocket, Louise took out her cell phone. She decided to call her sister, who lived only a few minutes away, knowing she would help and drive them all to the dentist. The children climbed out of the car, and Louise tried to contact her sister. The cell refused to work. Frustrated beyond words, Louise was baffled—the phone had been on charge all night. She could not think of a single reason why it should not work. As the time for the dental appointments had been and gone at this point, the only sensible thing to do, thought Louise, was to go back indoors, call the dental receptionist, apologize, and sit down for a calming drink. Into the house they went and took off their coats while Louise looked for the telephone number of the dentist. It was at that moment, they all became aware of something strange: it was an unfamiliar smell and what's more it was coming from the upper floor of the house. Dropping her address book, Louise ran upstairs toward the strong smell, which——she now recognized with fear——was smoke.

Opening the door of her spare bedroom, she was horrified to see black smoke billowing across the room. In an instant, she realized what had happened. Earlier that day, Louise had switched on an oil heater to warm the room in preparation for her aunt's visit the following day. There had been such a chill in the air and Louise was also airing the throw, which was draped on a bedside chair. The throw had slipped onto the heater and had slowly ignited! Switching the current off, Louise took care of the smoldering blanket and, now that all was safe, began to shake with delayed shock as the implication of what might have happened fully dawned on her.

Had the car started, they would have sped off to the dentist. Had the cell phone worked, they would have walked to the home of her sister close by. These actions would, of course, have left the house unattended, and the fire would have taken hold——with disastrous results. Eventually, when all was cleaned and straightened, Louise took the children into the kitchen to make the promised and much-needed drink. Suddenly, an idea formed in her mind. Louise tapped a number into her cell phone: it was working perfectly. Stepping into the garage with the car keys, she got in the car and turned the ignition key: it started at once. Amy, who had followed her into the garage, stared in disbelief and said, "Mommy, that is impossible!"

"I have only one explanation," Louise replied. "The angels insisted we return to the house and prevent a disaster. They were certainly looking after us throughout a very difficult day."

God Bless this house from site to stay,
From beam to wall, from end to end,
From ridge to basement, from balk to roof-tree,
From found to summit, found and summit.

FROM *CARMINA GADELICA*

divine key

To live in a truly expanding, prosperous, and creative way we must choose our words carefully and align with our spiritual self. Allow your angel of wisdom to fill your body, mind, and spirit constantly with vitality, comfort, and trust.

WISDOM AND PROTECTION

Angelic experiences, as we have seen, cover a wide range of types of intervention. Seeing an actual angel is the tip of an angelic iceberg. To see a large angel, in all its glory, I have discovered, is quite a rare event. We are far more likely to hear a voice, see a bright light, etc. This may be because few of us would be able to cope with the awesome sight of a large angel, and maybe most situations only rarely require such a dramatic vision. Oddly enough, several times when people have told me of seeing a large angel, it has often been during sessions of Reiki. The spiritual atmosphere engendered in such forms of healing appears to be conducive to attracting angels.

Raksha is normally a cheerful and confident character. She will happily give Reiki healing to anyone she feels to be in need. However, one day she found herself working in a treatment room in a house that was unfamiliar to her, where—for reasons she cannot fully explain—the atmosphere did not feel at all harmonious. In fact it all felt disturbingly negative. She was uneasy and felt decidedly vulnerable while administering Reiki to a lady on the treatment table in front of her. Something was very wrong, and Raksha was at a loss as to what it could be. Inexplicably, she felt the need for protection. Glancing up momentarily, she was astonished to see an angel standing at the end of the treatment table! This was an angel of biblical proportions: Raksha calculated the height of this magnificent being to be at least nine feet! It was the purest white, she says, with huge feathered wings, and the whole figure was surrounded by a golden glow, like an angel aura. A breathtaking sight although it was clear that other people in the room could not in fact see this angel. The heavenly visitor, it seems, was solely for Raksha and afforded the protection and love she was desperately in need of at that time.

"I have never seen the angel again," she told me. "I could not help but think that one such experience would be enough to last a lifetime!"

angel prayer

May the Angels watch over and protect me.
I seek the strength to be strong and renew a right spirit
within me.
Angels guide me in my heart, and in my home.

We have seen how God's wisdom, sent through his angels, has helped and rescued so many people, in so many ways in their daily lives. How often do we ignore that "inner feeling," the instinct telling us to follow the God-given wisdom? Children find it much easier to hear this inner voice; so, we should learn to listen and obey instinctively like they do. If we begin by practicing listening to the simple inner instincts we can move on to a more open acceptance of the fact that angel wisdom is there for us all, if only we would listen to it.

In ancient times it was firmly believed that the angels were responsible for putting the stars in their places and organizing the sun and moon to shine in turn. All this was to help man function in his daily life. Angels were, they believed, the font of all wisdom, and daily they gave thanks for their ministrations. Today, we may not believe that the angels place the stars in their orbits but few can doubt angelic wisdom and deliverance.

angel blessing

—◦◦◦◦—

*May the blessings of Divine clarity illuminate and
bring harmony in all areas of my life.*

My father explained this to me. "All things in this world," he
*said, "have souls or spirits. The sky has a spirit, the clouds have
spirits: the sun and moon have spirits, so have animals, trees,
grass, water, stars, everything."*

EDWARD GOODBIRD

∾ 4 ∾

angels of
joy and laughter

un and laughter are frequently seen in cases
of angelic intervention. The angels want us
to be happy, and we do not necessarily need
to be in trouble or in despair for them to
visit us. They can join us in the good times
too, sharing our joy and happiness, though this is a concept that
people often find hard to believe.

Frequently, when speaking in public, Gary and I have been
asked if we believe angels have a sense of humor. Without hesitation we always reply in the affirmative, firmly of the belief
that angels enjoy a joke as much as we mortals. Surely heaven
is a place of fun and happiness; indeed heaven without laughter
simply would not be heaven!

So many people tell us of lighthearted experiences, while
accounts abound of feelings of pure joy after angel visits. Our
first story happened some time ago, but it still makes Brian
chuckle to think about it.

FUN BEHIND BARS

It takes a special person to become a prison chaplain and certainly one needs a sense of humor. Thankfully, Brian has a real sense of fun, which helped to brighten life for his parishioners behind bars. On Sunday mornings, Brian would hold a service in his official capacity as chaplain in Parkhurst Prison's chapel. Congregation numbers fluctuated, and he never knew just how many people would attend. One Sunday morning there were considerably fewer men than usual filling the pews, resulting in the congregation being decidedly sparse. However, Brian knew that numbers were mainly down because of a very exciting football match being shown on television at the same time as his service.

Smiling broadly, Brian said, "As always, welcome to you all. Never mind the fact that numbers are depleted this morning— it is the quality that counts. Anyway, there is a host of angels sitting on that beam up there, joining us." Pointing upward to a large beam crossing the chapel, he noted that instinctively everyone looked up. Lifting a hymn book, Brian was just about to announce the first hymn, when a large white feather came floating down from the beam, gently rocking from side to side as it descended! Everyone burst out laughing.

It was of course most amusing, but, as Brian points out, there was no trace of a bird having been in the chapel, so he could only conclude that the angels were joining in the spirit of the morning and provoking laughter.

angel blessing

———— ⊷❦⊶ ————

O heavenly angels, I open the gates of joy and laughter.
My heart sings with living water and peace.
May this joy bring complete laughter into my soul.

ANGEL OF SURPRISE

It was the most glorious summer evening. The afternoon heat had subsided to leave a warm, balmy, fragrant breeze wafting through the open window. Mary sighed, she really did not feel like attending the evening service at the little village church, but felt a strong desire for company, so she went out. Living alone for most of her adult life, she could sometimes find days passing without speaking to anyone. This was especially true if her sister and family were away from home, as indeed they had been this past week. Cheerful faces would greet her at church, and there would be the chance of a good chat with people after the service as they walked home. Realizing that she would have to hurry or she would be late, Mary popped back into her little house to make sure the back door was secure and then hurried through the village, arriving just in time for the service to start.

Far from resenting the indoor service, Mary found herself fascinated by the address the vicar was preaching as it was about angels in our everyday lives. Pondering on the fact that she had never been aware of an angelic presence in any shape or form in her life, Mary wondered why this might be so, then concluded it could be her own fault—through not "tuning in," as it were. It certainly gave her a lot to think about, and she and her friends enjoyed talking about angels as they walked home.

Making a drink, Mary went into her lovely little garden and thought just how much she loved this time of year. It promised to be one of those marvelously clear nights, when the light would only fade late into the evening. Lots of people would still be out and about in their gardens until past 11 p.m., still enjoying the bright blue of the sky. At last Mary decided to go indoors, still thinking about angels and the vicar's address. Climbing the stairs, she became aware of a soft rustling noise, quite unfamiliar, which appeared to be coming from Mary's bedroom. Her mind immediately sprang to the subject of angels: could this be the gentle rustle of an angel's wings? Feeling happy and totally unafraid, Mary pushed open her bedroom door. A large, white face peered at her through the gathering gloom—it was her neighbor's cat!

Mary laughed out loud, realizing at once that this little furry visitor must have slipped into the house as she had returned to check the lock earlier. Chuckling to herself, Mary picked up the large cat and gave it a hug. Taking it downstairs, she gently placed it down on her doorstep telling it to go home. At this point, Mary gasped, "Well I never . . . I did have an angelic visitor after all!" You see, the cat's name on its tag was Angel.

angel meditation

Sit or lie comfortably in a dark area. Visualize yourself surrounded by a cloud of blue light energy. Open your mind and heart, and let your guardian angel of joy and laughter enter your body and mind.

Repeat silently through your meditation:

My heart sings with love for my Angel of Joy and Laughter.

Let the angelic energy flood your being. When you are ready, thank your guide and let yourself surface to the outer consciousness.

TIMELY INTERVENTION

The friendliest bookshop in Britain is surely Sweetens Bookshop, located in the bustling town of Bolton in the north of England. A warm, helpful atmosphere pervades, ensuring a busy scene of satisfied customers at all times. One morning, shortly after opening time, the staff received a phone call from the BBC. Currently filming a documentary program about the public's reading and book-purchasing habits, they wanted to come along later that morning and film inside the shop. It would be interesting, they said, to observe the types of books arousing interest, and they would particularly like to interview a customer if possible. Well, being Britain's friendliest book-shop, the staff said yes of course. The television team was due to arrive at 11 a.m., usually a very busy time, and so the staff busied themselves, making everything look tidy and especially attractive.

The two intervening hours passed quickly, and soon they were just moments away from 11 a.m. All was ready except for one vital ingredient: people! The shop had not had a single customer the entire morning! No one could recall this ever happening before and it would be totally embarrassing to have a film unit from the BBC arrive only to find not a customer in sight, but what on earth could they do? Looking through the window, Debe, one of the assistants, saw the film crew appear outside. At that moment, she realized, she was in fact standing in front of a display of my books. Touching one, she remarked to a colleague, "We could use one of Glennyce's angels!"

Into the shop came the film crew with all their equipment, but immediately following them—to the staff's astonish-ment—was a crowd of people. In seconds the shop was full! For the whole of the two hours that the film crew was present, the shop continued to welcome customers in unprecedented numbers. Business was brisk and the film crew was delighted.

The icing on the cake was the arrival of a friend of Debe's who had simply been in the area and thought that she would drop by. Articulate and elegant, she was only too happy to be inter-viewed by the television people. The event was all extremely successful, and when the television crew packed their things, they thanked the Sweetens staff profusely for a very interesting session. Within minutes of the crew's, the shop became empty once more. A hush descended where moments before there had been hectic bustle—it was quite beyond belief.

The following morning, I visited the shop and Debe greeted me with a laugh, saying, "We have a good story to tell you!" The staff, delighted at yesterday's events, thought it was marvelous that the angel had solved their problem, although they had all enjoyed a good laugh. I replied that I felt sure the shop had its own angel who was chuckling too!

The angels laughed,
God looked down from his seventh heaven and smiled.
The angels spread their wings and,
Together with Elijah, flew upwards into the sky.

ISAAC BASHEVIS SINGER

SYNCHRONICITY TO MAKE YOU SMILE

Another title for this story might be "The Luck of the Irish" because our story begins on the Emerald Isle. Norman and his wife, Jean, had planned a trip of a lifetime. They were setting off from their home in Ireland around the world to visit many exotic locations. Arriving at each wonderful destination, they planned to hire a car and explore. When asked later what he remembered most about this journey, Norman replied, "A bout of hiccups!" This might take some explaining, especially as the couple saw spellbinding scenery and met many wonderful people on their travels. I shall give you the background to Norman's amusing remark as Norman gave it to me.

Many years ago, back in the 1950s, Norman was a keen rugby player. The team coach was a wonderful character called Dr. Dick Ongley, known to everyone as Tubby. He hailed from Wellington, New Zealand, and was hugely popular—full of fun, Norman says—with a roguish and infectious sense of humor and an enthusiasm for life. Everybody, especially Norman and his family, was dreadfully sad when Tubby announced that he and his family would be returning to New Zealand. The friends kept in touch sporadically, and it was with great sadness they learned of Tubby's death years later. It was then, when Norman and Jean embarked on their exciting journey, that they resolved to try to find some of Tubby's family. At this point, they had no contact address but knew that his wife and three daughters were still living somewhere in New Zealand.

Traveling through South Island, Norman made many inquiries about Dr. Ongley along the way. Knowing how keen all New Zealanders are about rugby, he felt sure someone would have information regarding the doctor's family. They drew a complete blank, however. Unfortunately, when they arrived at the ferry taking them to North Island, the weather determined that they would bypass Wellington, missing a chance to look in the last known location of their friend. It was almost Christmas, so Norman and his wife, who were behind schedule, pressed on with their journey.

Finding themselves in the small town of Waikanae, they

stopped the car, intending to buy supplies that would enable them to drive north all Christmas Day. Noticing a large super-market, they pulled off the road into the busy parking lot. Shoppers, carolers, and a distinct lack of parking spaces greeted them. After a long search, they found a parking spot.

Fascinated by the goods on sale in the crowded store, they made their way with difficulty through the crowds. Suddenly, they were both amused by a very pretty baby who was sitting in her mother's shopping cart and, as Norman said, was "hiccup-ping as loud as a cuckoo!" Laughing, they chatted with the little girl's mother. The baby was called Emma and her poor mother had no idea what had precipitated the bout of hiccups. Saying their good-byes, Norman and Jean made their way through the throng to their car once more. Imagine their surprise, when there, just a few cars away in this enormous parking lot, were little Emma and her mother, packing away their groceries.

Jean could not resist another chat with this delightful young mother and baby, so Norman attended to the groceries while Jean went to speak to her. Then he heard his wife shout, "Come here, Norman!" His wife explained that the young lady's mother had been born in their hometown in Ireland, Clontarf.

"What was your mother's name?" Norman asked.

"Ongley," came the startling reply! It became clear that baby Emma was Tubby's great-granddaughter; her mother, Fiona, was Tubby's granddaughter, and her mother, Patricia, was Tub-by's eldest daughter! What a Christmas present, it was quite unbelievable. Contact had been made after all that time.

This amazing synchronicity raised more than a few smiles, and today Norman and Jean still find the episode hard to believe. I like to think that Tubby had something to do with it, and I can imagine him smiling warmly down from heaven.

> And yet, as angels in some brighter dreams,
> Call to the soul when man doth sleep.

HENRY VAUGHN

ANGELS AND DREAMS

Sad though she was to be leaving her native Toronto, Christine could not help but be excited by the prospect of living in England. The first sixteen years of Christine's life had been spent among family and friends in a city she loved, and the thought of saying good-bye was not a happy one. One of the hardest farewells would be to her best friend Caroline; they would miss each other dreadfully. When the time finally came, the move was full of joy and sorrow, the sadness tinged with thoughts of their new life and how exciting that would be. Christine's father had been sent to London by his employer initially for a period of two years. Settling down did take a while. However, Christine soon made new friends and began to enjoy the bustling city of London.

The years passed, and Christine's father announced that the position in London was in fact permanent if they so wished it to be. It was decided that they would stay, having adopted the city as their own at this point. Keeping in touch with friends and family in Canada was initially smooth and easy, but inevitably several contacts were lost as the years rolled by. Sadly, one of the friends who eventually lost touch was Caroline. Their letters had become less frequent as both girls were obviously moving on. From time to time, Christine would think about her friend and wonder how she was. The last letter she sent, however, did not receive an answer and Christine assumed that Caroline's family must have moved away from their old address.

Ten years later and Christine was not only grown up but was planning her wedding. Everything was in order: the beautiful local church, the reception venue, and the honeymoon location. The wedding was to be immediately before Christmas, on Christine's twenty-sixth birthday to be precise, and so the young couple thought the honeymoon should be spent somewhere warm. They decided on Tunisia; it was exotic-sounding and they could be sure of sunshine. The day before the wedding Christine found herself thinking again of her childhood friend Caroline, wishing she could share her news and hoping that she too was very happy with her life.

The wedding day itself was perfect, cold and bright and made extra special by the fact that several relatives had flown from Canada to be present. It was truly a happy occasion and the following morning was also great fun as the whole family traveled with the newlyweds to Heathrow Airport to wave good-bye and wish them well.

Tunisia was everything they had expected—full of color and beautiful architecture—and the hotel was simply lovely. Christine and her new husband spent the first day drinking in all the sights and sounds of this beautiful country. On the second night in their hotel, Christine had a very vivid dream. It featured Caroline, who was smiling and telling her how happy she was to hear about the wedding. Waking the next morning, Christine told her husband about the dream: "It was incredibly clear," she said. "Even the clothes she was wearing were bright and distinct in every detail."

"It was because you had been thinking about her," Christine's husband replied. Wishing Caroline could have been at the wedding, Christine agreed but felt the old pang of sadness return as she thought about her friend. But it promised to be a beautiful day, so they changed the conversation to where to go after breakfast. Cheerfully closing the bedroom door, they made their way to the dining hall. There was a sight Christine will never forget, for sitting at the nearest table to the door was Caroline! The girls recognized each other instantly, as neither had changed very much facially, though both were taller.

What a grand reunion it was, with shared tears of joy and many hugs. Caroline could scarcely believe it when Christine told her about the dream. Without hesitation she laughed and said, "The angels are working overtime!"

"Well, after all their hard work," Christine replied, "we must make sure not to lose each other again," and they have kept to their word.

When we give out positive thoughts and love, the angels catch and carry them away to others. Giving out joy and laughter will make the angels' task much happier and their ability to touch your heart, a simple matter. We hope the following exercise attracts the angel of laughter to you.

guiding light insight

Angels may bring out the best qualities in our relationships and are attracted to laughter or a childlike energy. Angelic laughter is a response to the pure joy of being present and alive.

To invoke your angel of joy and laughter, repeat three times:

Guardian Angel of Joy and Laughter, come to me. I call upon my guide for complete joy and laughter.

THE LAST LAUGH

How people manage to retain a sense of humor in the face of a terminal illness I shall never know, but one very brave lady managed this remarkable feat. Pamela was just thirty-seven years old, a wife and mother of two small children, when she discovered that she was terminally ill. Strong and determined, she amazed everyone with her fortitude. Pamela's good friend Irene told me how humor and courage never failed Pamela at this dreadful time.

Family and friends would try to help in any way they could and, as a healer, Irene would visit in this capacity. Irene describes herself as a "hands-on intuitive healer." Many people, Irene says, practice a form of hands-on healing. This may be Reiki or spiritual healing, but "intuitive" is the word that best describes Irene's work, which complements and supplements medical care. These healing sessions enabled Pamela to find peace, stillness, and the strength to face death.

After Pamela had died, the instructions she had left for funeral arrangements were read and considered. The funeral was to take place in her large parish church and would be a dignified and moving service. However, Pamela had requested that Irene should take part in the service—a concept that Irene did not exactly relish. She was not at all used to speaking in such circumstances, and especially not alongside a Church of England dignitary, so she concluded that perhaps this was Pamela's sense of humor coming through! If this was Pamela's wish, Irene thought, then she would indeed speak at the service.

The day arrived and the service was lovely, moving, and inspiring, just as Pamela had been. However, during the service Irene had a growing concern. The microphone she would have to use when speaking to the congregation presented a problem. This had clearly been adjusted for the vicar, a very tall individual, while Irene struggled to reach a mere five feet! Eventually, it was Irene's turn to speak and she gingerly approached the microphone. It was way above her head, and a murmur rippled through the church. At this point, without warning, two amazing things happened. The altar candles, having burned to a small, low flame at this point, as time was running out, suddenly shot high into the air and the microphone slid down the stand completely unaided, halting immediately in front of Irene's face! The murmur became full-blown laughter, and Irene said silently, "Thank you, Pamela."

After the service had ended, the man who had been in charge of the sound equipment told Irene that he was baffled. Unaware that she was going to be speaking, he had fixed the microphone to accommodate the vicar. But aware that it could potentially be embarrassing to have the microphone slide when speaking, he had tightened the adjuster with a spanner, so there was no way, he explained, that it could have moved without similar pressure. Irene chuckled again. "God bless Pamela," she said, "for having the last laugh!"

angel affirmations

I am joyously receiving loving-kindness.
My life flows easily and effortlessly.
I live in the now.

MESSAGE OF JOY

The following story is in fact a trilogy: first, it's Belinda's story; second, Therese's story; and third, there is the conclusion. It is a fascinating and inspiring account of friendship and intervention by the angels.

belinda

Belinda lives in Vanderbijlpark, South Africa. A wife and mother of two small children, she had studied engineering at a university, but her faith had given her a strong desire to help as many people as possible. Life had not been easy for Belinda, and yet she prayed for a gift to enable her to help others. The gift she received was one she could never have imagined in her wildest dreams, and it has transformed her life. One day the entire family, without warning, became ill simultaneously with scarlet fever. Belinda said they all lay in bed in a row, incapable of helping each other. It was at this point that Belinda's prayers began to be answered. She became aware of angels hovering above the family's heads and was even given their names. Peace pervaded the room and filled Belinda with a wonderful sense of calm. She discovered with surprise that she could in fact communicate with these angels at this point and, amazingly, received answers to her questions. This was a miracle for Belinda, and she thanked God for this wonderful gift. Workshops followed and Belinda has enabled so many people to receive angelic messages, often with life-changing results, that she feels truly blessed.

therese

Therese longed for a family, but it clearly was not going to be easy. After years of yearning and simply hoping it would happen one day, she finally decided to seek medical intervention. Various distinguished experts supervised tests and treatments for several years, all without success, so Therese's situation was looking pretty hopeless.

Quite by accident, Therese met an old friend of her sister's who was pregnant. Talking to Therese about this, she divulged that she had prayed hard for this much-wanted baby. It was at that point that Therese decided she would also ask for intervention from God, and so she began to pray, asking if divine help would be given her.

Old friends, Belinda and Therese met after many years of only sparse communication. Imagine Therese's surprise when Belinda told her friend that the angels had sent a message for her—to tell her that she would soon have a baby son! The message also added that she would be given confidence and awareness of her inner strength, which was greater than she ever realized. The message was, of course, bewildering and Therese did not know what to make of it at all. She took some time before plucking up the courage to tell her husband of these surprising events. Oddly, whenever Therese reread this message, the month "April" would come into her head. It was now January and Therese was due to start a course of IVF treatment—a big and very expensive step. Therese wondered what she should do: had she sufficient faith to leave all this in God's hands? Another message came from the angels via Belinda, which said that there was no need for treatment; trust, and all would be well.

For the first time in her life, Therese had a vision. It portrayed a baby dressed in blue and her husband standing by her side. She looked down at this lovely little being and could actually see his face. It was, she says, "clear as daylight," and she felt so very blessed.

Shortly after these amazing events, tests confirmed that Therese was indeed pregnant! Not long after this book was finished, I received a "stop-the-press" piece of news. Therese has delivered safely a little boy called Jason Jaco. I am sure the angels are smiling with us all at this wonderful news. A special gift after so much yearning and sorrow. Faith, prayer, and the angels have truly blessed this new family.

conclusion

Belinda wrote to me, giving some additional background information to this story. For some time now, she has been receiving messages from the angels. She hears the messages in her head and writes them down in a mode of automatic writing. Her story, however, goes back some ten years, when Belinda was attending university, studying engineering. She shared an apartment with her close friend Therese, but sadly the stress of the intense course started to tell on Belinda's normally easy-going personality. The volume of work began to make her feel depressed, and life became a struggle. Sadly, her friend decided that she could no longer share the accommodations. It was not a happy parting and left both women feeling uneasy.

The years passed and the friends only exchanged e-mails on birthdays or similar occasions, neither knowing what to say on the telephone. It was odd, living in the same town and never even bumping into each other. One day, Belinda's husband bumped into her friend's husband, learning only that the couple had no children. Belinda assumed they were concentrating on their careers. Out of the blue, Belinda received an e-mail from Therese suggesting that they meet up for a cup of tea and a chat. This was such an unusual request, that Belinda realized it must mean that the angels would be sending a message for her friend. It had been only recently that the messages had started, but Belinda knew instinctively that this had to be part of the reason for her friend's contact. They arranged to meet at a place where Belinda's children could happily play while the friends chatted. Sure enough, an angel message came through, and it was that Belinda's friend would have a little baby son. Belinda of course, had no idea that a baby was so badly wanted by the couple and had no idea how her friend would react to the message.

The meeting was wonderful and very emotional, with ten years of news to catch up on. It was with surprise that Belinda learned her friend had been hoping and trying for years to have a child. That very morning, she had asked God for a sign whether she should resign herself to never being a mother. At this point, Belinda told her friend about the messages she received, handing her the piece of paper containing news about a baby. Her friend was overwhelmed, and understandably, slightly disbelieving. As the two friends parted they hugged and found themselves in tears; the past melted away and they were firm friends again. Belinda had a strong feeling of divine guidance and left for home contented.

Continuing with her program of tests and treatment, Belinda's friend called one day asking if there might be another angel message soon. She was in fact undecided as to what course, if any, she should continue with. There would be no need, Belinda said. Simply trust. A little while later, the message from the angels was to say the time was right. Calling her friend, Belinda asked Therese if there was any news. "No, why do you ask?" came the response.

"I think you should have a pregnancy test," Belinda stated, but her friend was too nervous to take the required action. Two weeks later, she had an official blood test at the hospital and was told to her sheer delight and amazement that she was indeed pregnant! It was such a miraculous, joyful event, that Belinda's friend knew for certain all would be well, and that the baby would be born healthy. She even had a vision of herself and her husband holding the child. "It has been so wonderful to be part of this miracle," says Belinda, who fervently hopes that many more lives will be changed through her ability to receive messages from the angels.

We receive more letters about white feathers than any other form of angel signal. Everyone today, it seems, is aware that the "calling card" of an angel is the lovely white feather. It is a gentle way of saying that the angels are there, watching over us, comforting and encouraging us in our daily lives. This was certainly the case for Suzannah, for whom finding her first feather changed her life.

FIRST FEATHER

The end of term was rapidly approaching, and Suzannah knew that her teacher husband would be more than ready for a break.

The Easter holidays would be an ideal time to get out of the city and relax in a more rural setting. They decided to spend a few days in the little town of Telford, set in the beautiful county of Shropshire. The weather was perfect, warm with deep blue skies, and the location ideal. The river Teme runs through Telford, and one morning Suzannah and her husband decided to walk along the banks.

A hugely talented singer/songwriter with considerable international success behind her, Suzannah had nevertheless found herself unwilling to compose or sing for some time. A strong sense of "being on the wrong track" pervaded her thoughts and she found herself wondering just where her musical life was heading. Recently, her strong faith in God and her belief in angels had led her to explore some more spiritual dimensions of music. After reading my book *Teen Angel*, Suzannah found herself drawn to one particular story, and was indeed moved to compose a song. It was, she says, the best work she had accomplished in some time, and the resulting CD is spine-chillingly beautiful.

Walking along the riverbank was a truly lovely experience that day. The morning was so quiet, with scarcely a soul in sight, and the air was perfectly still. Suddenly, and instinctively, Suzannah and her husband stopped walking. A strange compulsion made her look up and then catch her breath: directly overhead, a huge white feather floated down, resting finally at her feet. It was a magical moment, no bird in sight or disturbance of the still air. Suzannah found herself wondering whether this beautiful feather could really be for her, deciding eventually to leave it there as a gift to share with others.

Shortly afterward, Suzannah was contacted by a music company in the United States. It transpired that they were delighted with the song "Teen Angel" and would be happy to be her overseas distributor! There could be no doubt in Suzannah's mind that her new spiritually orientated path in music had been endorsed that day on holiday by the angel gift. She decided that in future she would trust angels implicitly to guide her along life's path.

THE CHRISTMAS ANGEL

For most of us, Christmas and joy go hand in hand. For Steve in particular the Christmas of 2002 brought joy in abundance. It was December 23 and very cold when Steve received a call to repair a boiler. This was Steve's specialty but he knew only too well that it might be a simple task or very complicated, depending on the fault or type of boiler. Arriving at the house, Steve inspected the boiler, and after making several adjustments, he realized that in fact the problem was now even worse! His heart sank: this was indeed a complicated problem. He realized at this point that what he actually required was a printed circuit board.

Seeing my blank stare when telling me his story, Steve patiently explained the problem. There are, he assured me, hundreds of different types of circuit boards that can be fitted into boilers. Each individual boiler is different and of varying type, making it unlikely that an engineer would have the correct circuit board in hand. In addition to this problem, however, is the fact that these printed boards are very expensive, costing possibly hundreds of pounds each. They are therefore ordered when needed and not carried around in most heating engineers' vans.

All this was very depressing. Steve was faced with the unenviable task of telling the people who had called on him for help that they would be without hot water or heat for the whole of Christmas. It could, he informed me, often take several weeks to obtain the part required. Staring at the boiler Steve tried to think of how he could help these people. He did have a large heater at home he could loan them, but that would not solve the hot water problem, which was insoluble. Placing his hand on the boiler, he said aloud, "Please angels, I need your help desperately!" Nothing happened.

Chuckling at this point, he said he had almost expected a flashing blue light and the boiler to spring to life! Slowly he packed away his tools and carried them downstairs to his van. I shall put these away, he thought, and then I simply will have to face these people and break the awful news. Placing his main tools in the back of the van, he then went around to the side door and slowly slid it open. At this point, he received the shock of his life: falling out of the van, directly into his hands, was the exact circuit board he needed!

Climbing the stairs once more to the top of the house, in complete disbelief, he tried the circuit board, and yes, incredibly, it was the correct one. In minutes the job was complete. The couple smiled happily when told all was well, never knowing of Steve's dilemma. Sitting in his van, after leaving the house, too shocked to start the engine, Steve took stock of the situation once more. He had never in his professional career stored expensive circuit boards in his van, or anywhere else for that matter. How on earth could the exact board he required have fallen into his hands at the eleventh hour, so to speak? Well, he did know of course: there may not have been any flashing lights, but the angels had heard him after all. Grinning to himself, he silently thanked them, realizing the true meaning of Christmas joy that year.

There is a footnote to this lovely story. Steve and his partner, Joan, own an alternative health center in North Manchester, and I was visiting them specifically to get the details of Steve's story. We sat in the shop, surrounded by statues of angels, crystals, etc., as I wrote down the details. Finally, I said, "Did the people in the house ever know the facts of this story?"

"No," replied Steve, "sadly I have never seen them since." At that very moment the lady involved in the story walked past the window! Steve dashed out and asked her to come inside, where he related the incredible events of that Christmas to a very surprised shopper.

angel prayer

Almighty Angelic hosts, bring your joyous voices, and beloved songs to my soul.
I accept your guidance and welcome the presence of angels in my everyday life.

AMAZING BUT TRUE

I am sure that many people reading this book will be familiar with the beautiful song "Scarlet Ribbons" sung by Harry Belafonte. The song, you will recall, tells of a father praying that his daughter might have the scarlet ribbons she desperately longs for. Inexplicably the next morning, they appear on her pillow. Very sweet but a fairy story you might think. However, I have been surprised recently by several letters telling me how after prayer, or imploring angels for help, objects really did appear.

During a radio phone-in as the guest of James Whale, a caller related a story to me about a minister of religion in New Zealand. He had apparently asked people to share a meal in his home even though there was no food in the house. He and his wife prayed before answering a knock on the door. Opening it they could scarcely believe their eyes: a huge basket of food lay there. Miles away from the city, deep in the country, no one simply "passed by" and there was not a soul in sight. Shortly after the program, I received several letters assuring me that it was not a unique event. I shall relate just one of the stories told to me by a lady called Louise.

Life was proving to be a bit of a struggle for Louise. Widowed at the early age of thirty-four, she found herself almost penniless. Her little girl, Rosie, was about to have her fourth birthday. Louise was depressed at the thought, knowing it would be a rather bleak day for Rosie. Financial problems compounded her grief, as Louise had sadly been forced to move from a comfortable house into a tiny apartment. A small group of friends from Rosie's little school had been invited for a birthday tea, and Louise thought she could just about afford this if she baked a cake herself. There would be no spare change for a gift from her though, and this distressed Louise. Rosie longed for a duvet cover and curtains for her bedroom, featuring Paddington Bear. Whenever Louise gently tried to tell her she could not possibly afford them, Rosie laughed, convinced this was a game her mother was playing.

The night before her birthday, Rosie was excited and happy, telling her mother that the old, faded duvet cover would be replaced with her lovely new one the next day. Louise groaned inwardly and, kissing her daughter good night, she went slowly back to the little sitting room, where she started to cry. This is all too much, she sobbed to herself, I cannot cope. For the first time, she found herself talking to her husband, saying out loud, "I am sure you are an angel now, can you please help?"

Instantly tears turned to giggles. The very idea made her laugh—how could her deceased husband, even though he might be an angel, purchase a set of Paddington Bear covers! Telling me this story, Louise chuckled. "I thought I had lost my mind!" Sinking into bed, she was so weary with anxiety that she fell into a deep sleep.

Waking early, Louise tiptoed into the kitchen and lifted the cake she had decorated from the fridge, placing it on the kitchen table. This cake was to be a surprise for Rosie when she woke. It was in the shape of Paddington Bear, of course, and Louise was rather proud of it. The trundle of the garbage truck could be heard outside the apartment, and Louise realized she needed to place her trash can outside for collection. Pulling on her coat, she went outside.

To her surprise, leaning against the trash can was a large cardboard box. Where on earth did that come from, she thought, bending down to pick it up. Finding it to be a little heavy, she wheeled her trash can to the gate and then, lifting the box, carried it inside for a closer look. Placing it on a kitchen chair, she opened it gingerly. Inside was a brand-new pair of bedroom curtains, a duvet cover, and pillowcase, all featuring Paddington Bear! Louise was shaking as she stared into the open box. It was incredible, impossible. Thoughts of "how?" or "who?" whirled through her head. Tears sprang to her eyes once more, this time with joy. Whatever the explanation, her angel had answered; now all she had to do was to say thank you.

angel blessing

May the blessings of happiness, love, and abundance, radiate within.

Clearly, healing is granted in many forms, from physical strength to peace of mind, relieving worry and tension in our lives. The problem may be major and life-threatening or a small trouble, which nevertheless disturbs us. Once more we must trust and ask the angels, who demonstrated their power of healing in the stories we have just read.

5

angels of perception

ithout the guidance of true perception and vision nothing would be successful. True perception occurs when our small, everyday selves connect to our Higher Selves. When this happens, our angels will give us the knowledge, insight, and divine truth that we need to heal and create in our lives.

Everyone is familiar with the expression "seeing the light" and most of us realize that this can mean seeing in many forms, not simply visual but clarity in terms of thought and emotional understanding. Realizing this, we decided to call this chapter after the angel of perception because of the myriad ways in which angels see and respond to our need for help. Not only do they find the most appropriate method of intervening, such as appearing in everyday dress, through music, a voice, touch, light, etc., but many appear to have embraced modern technology as viable means of communication. Cameras, clocks, cell phones,

CD players, answering machines, and even computers have registered messages that are impossible to explain by rational methods. Symbolism and synchronicity, especially spiritual in nature, also feature in many remarkable angel stories. In this chapter, we have included just a few of the hundreds of stories we have received documenting these amazing experiences.

Angels exist through the eyes of faith, and faith is perception.
Only if you can perceive it can you experience it.

JOHN WESTERHOFF

angel blessing

O heavenly angels, I open the gates of perception.
My heart sings with living water and peace.
May this perception bring complete laughter into my soul.

AN UNLIKELY ANGEL

Teenagers and turbulence are practically synonymous, and just when growing up seems to be at its most painful, along come exams. At seventeen Craig was experiencing the most stress-ful time he could ever remember. Life was a trial and here he was in the middle of important exams—what could possibly be worse. One afternoon, after an exam, Craig was on the verge of panic, trying to determine whether his answers had met the required standard.

Walking slowly through the city toward home, Craig turned into a narrow road running between a church and a graveyard, a long, quiet passageway, along which he walked deep in thought. Looking up he saw coming toward him an old lady so disheveled in appearance that Craig thought she might be a bag lady. Walking past this old lady, Craig was taken by surprise when she turned toward him and said, "Jesus loves you!"

Craig says words fail him at this point in the story to describe the wave of inner peace that flooded over him at that moment, bringing a sense of total calm. It was a unique experience, and Craig knew instantly this was no ordinary old lady. He was actually too surprised to say thank you initially, but shortly after regaining his composure, he turned to speak to the lady, only to find she was nowhere to be seen! The long, narrow passage was completely empty. He was now totally speechless but also content in the wonderful reassuring feeling of peace.

Sometime later Craig wrote to me, asking if I considered this was his angel, although deep down inside he knew this to be the case. I smiled when I read his words "I am perfectly sane, not madly religious in any way." This is so typical of people who have experienced angels in everyday clothing. Not wishing to be thought strange in any way, they may wonder if their mind was playing tricks on them, but really they know that the heart feels the truth. Their very reaction confirms how normal they are, and Craig was simply a troubled and stressed teenager, longing for peace of mind.

Looking back, Craig says his angel visitation was a profoundly positive episode in his life. He very kindly and bravely said that he is more than happy to share it with others. Welcomed by such an open feeling of acceptance, I feel certain that Craig's angel will be close to him for life.

ANGEL IN DISGUISE

Frequently angels appear to people in the form of a loved one, ensuring they do not cause fear or alarm. This seems to be particularly true in encounters with children or the elderly. Marie told me the story about the day a special angel appeared to her ninety-four-year-old mother.

Every Thursday at exactly 12 noon, Marie would visit her mother. She would bring a hot meal with her and was always prepared to help in any way that her mother might require. Parking her car at the front of the house, on this occasion Marie looked up, expecting to see her mother's face smiling down from the window and her little dog barking a greeting as usual. Today, however, all was silent and there was no face looking down at her. Knocking on the door brought no response, so with mounting anxiety Marie ran to the back of the house, repeatedly knocking and peering though the window, but there simply was no sign of her mother.

Her mother's next-door neighbor appeared at his front door to ask if there was a problem. Marie told him the situation and added that she was going to hurry a few doors down the road to where a friend had an emergency key to the house. Typically, and to Marie's distress, the neighbor with the spare key was not at home. Turning to dash back to her mother's house, where the next-door neighbor stood waiting, she saw him wave excitedly. Apparently a young man had just opened the front door and walked out, rushing away before the startled neighbor could say anything.

Marie hurried inside and, to her relief, found her mother lying on the lounge sofa, her little dog quietly by her side. It was obvious that she had suffered a fall: her hands were shaking and her knees cut and bruised. Bending over her mother, Marie held her hand and tried to establish just what had happened. Apparently, her mother had been upstairs in her bedroom when, looking through the window, she had seen her daughter's car approaching. Hurrying to get down the stairs, she must have lost her footing and fallen. Lying at the bottom of the stairs she was unable to get up and could not be seen through any of the windows. "What a good job Alex arrived in time to help me," she told Marie. "He picked me up and carried me to the sofa."

Marie was decidedly taken aback. Alex was her son and, of course, her mother's grandson, but he lived at least sixty miles away. It transpired afterward that he had not been anywhere near his grandmother's that morning, just as Marie suspected.

Trying to make sense of this incident, Marie took stock. The back door was firmly locked from the inside, so no one had entered or exited that way. The next-door neighbor said the young man had left the house via the front door and seemed to have disappeared when he turned to see where he had gone. Moreover, the little dog had not barked once, which was totally out of character, as normally the problem was to get him to be quiet when a visitor arrived! Usually this little dog had to be restrained from running out of the door as soon as it opened, having never learned the concept of road safety, and yet there he sat calm and still next to Marie's mother.

The only possible explanation, Marie felt sure, had to be a most welcome angel, who had appeared in a guise familiar to her old mother. Today, ninety-six years of age, Marie's mother is still happy and independent, living in her little house. Marie also is happy, secure in the knowledge that a very special guardian angel watches over her.

angel meditation

Sit or lie comfortably in a dark area. Visualize yourself surrounded by a cloud of blue light energy. Open your mind and heart, and let your guardian angel of perception enter.

Repeat silently through your meditation:

My heart sings with love for my Angel of Perception.

Let the angelic energy take over your being. When you are ready, thank your guide and let yourself surface to outer consciousness.

TIME TO REFLECT

It has often crossed my mind when visiting the hairdresser, how the stylist's feet and back must ache at the end of the day. Working very long hours frequently seems to be an occupational hazard, and even the fittest person must become weary. Imagine trying to cope with such a job if suffering from a disabling condition such as multiple sclerosis. This was precisely what Margaret was struggling with on a daily basis. She was the owner of a busy hairdressing salon and worked alongside her staff each day. A strong, determined, and lovely lady, Margaret simply did not want to bow to the inevitable and retire from the work she loved. Each day became increasingly difficult and the drive home presented several problems. One of the most challenging obstacles occurred when Margaret came to a halt outside her own front door. Her house is rather low in comparison to the road. Steep steps lead down to the front door and even though there is a sturdy handrail, it was not an easy task. Reaching the top of the steps after leaving the car could often be a problem for Margaret, as there was the wide pavement to negotiate before reaching the relative safety of the handrail.

It was the beginning of March and, true to the saying, the month was coming in like a lion. Strong winds and a touch of ice on the pavements caused Margaret's heart to sink as she returned home one evening. Pulling herself from her car and locking the door took a huge effort, and she leaned against her car in despair. The space between the car and the handrail seemed enormous; the pavement was icy and the wind blew her off guard. David, Margaret's husband, was terribly worried about her and had pleaded with her to retire, fearing just such an occasion. Margaret's eyes stung with tears as she realized he was right. Holding on to the car as best she could for support, she tried to get her cell phone from her coat pocket. Maybe a neighbor would be home and able to help. At this point, a car passed her, suddenly stopping in front of hers, and a man got out, swiftly rushing to Margaret's side. "Are you all right?" he asked. With such relief at seeing him, Margaret replied, "No I am not. Could you please help me?"

The man was rather oddly dressed, all in black—perhaps a robe, she thought on reflection. He had a white collar, similar to a clerical one, making it quite an unusual outfit all together. All that mattered at that moment, however, was that help was at hand, and Margaret was full of gratitude that he had come to her aid. When he took her arm, the most amazing thing happened. A sensation she had never experienced before filled her with a warm glow like love, flowing through and around her. The man's eyes were a bright piercing blue and seemed to transfix Margaret with his gaze. It was, she said, "simply phenomenal." Relating this story, some three years later, Margaret struggled to find the words to describe the sensations and became emotional, as the feelings of that night stirred once more as if the incident had happened only yesterday.

Returning to her story, she told me that by now she was in a daze but, held by this amazing stranger, managed to cope with the first few steps. Eventually her strength and confidence returned as she managed to secure a firm grip on the handrail.

Calmness enveloped her, as she said, "Thank you so much. I can manage the rest of the way alone now." Smiling, he released her arm, nodding encouragement. Margaret turned to watch him go up the steps intending to say thank you again, but astonishingly, there was no one there! The steps, pavement, and entire length of the street were deserted, and what is more the car had vanished. That is impossible, she uttered to herself. No one could have reached the top of the stone steps in an instant and, even had that been possible, she would surely have seen him on the pavement, or heard him starting his car.

Reaching the front door of her house, Margaret slowly walked into the warmth but found herself overcome with emotion. The tears flowed as she instantly understood what had happened: her very own angel had come to her rescue. There was a message also, she says, in this encounter, for she feels sure that the angel's presence enabled her to decide that the time had come to retire from work and look after herself.

ANGEL IN THE FAST LANE

The traffic on the highway that morning was the heaviest Paula could ever remember. It appeared that for most people hurtling along at speeds far exceeding the permitted limit had become the norm in their effort to get to work. The volume of cars and heavy trucks on her route appeared to increase daily, and Paula too was driving fast. Perilous conditions indeed, but the danger increased dramatically with the frightening events that followed. Having been traveling at approximately eighty-five miles an hour, Paula realized that she was losing speed and power fast. There was no apparent reason for this, as her foot was still pressed down on the accelerator and the dashboard display did not indicate a problem of any kind. At this point, driving in the outside lane, Paula realized that she was in serious trouble.

The car continued to lose speed and amazingly Paula was able to cut across the swiftly moving traffic lanes via timely gaps, which miraculously opened up, before she reached the hard shoulder. Pulling in and stopping, Paula wondered what her next course of action should be. Immediately there was a loud bang and one of her tires exploded! Shaking with fright, Paula was at a loss as to what to do next. She was reluctant to leave her vehicle, owing to the narrowness of the hard shoulder and the speed of the passing traffic.

Within seconds, a young man appeared and without a word began to change Paula's tire. Gingerly stepping away from her car, she gazed in awe as he swiftly completed the task. Shocked and bewildered, Paula simply stared and could not find her voice. The new tire was fitted with incredible speed and the young man simply walked away without a word. Waking as if from a nightmare, Paula turned to shout thank you after the man, only to find that there was no trace of him.

It was some time later, when she finally arrived at work that she tried to analyze the events. The car had been in perfect working order, full of gas and with no other signs of a fault. What, then, had made the car slowly lose speed, alerting her to the fact that she must make her way to the hard shoulder? Imagine the catastrophe that might have occurred had the tire burst in the fast lane; Paula shuddered to think of the consequences.

Second, where had the young man appeared from so swiftly, and what made him change the tire with almost supernatural speed and strength? It certainly was a mystery. There did not appear to be a rational solution, and Paula concluded that the angels had been with her in one form or another at that most dangerous of times.

Angels and ministers of faith defend us.

WILLIAM SHAKESPEARE

THE MESSENGER

With her little golden head bent intently over the sand, it had taken Emily at least half an hour to build her wonderful castle, although clearly it was not finished yet. Fiona smiled, watching her daughter through the kitchen window. What a brilliant idea it had been, she thought, to make Emma a sandpit at the bottom of the garden. Shortly, when the cakes came out of the oven, she would take Emma one to eat, along with a drink for herself, and then she would sit outside for a while enjoying the afternoon.

Turning to check the cakes in the oven, Fiona was surprised by a loud voice calling her name from the garden. Jumping with surprise she dashed back to the window, only to find nothing had changed: Emma was still happily building in the sandpit, and there was no sign of anyone else in the garden. Mystified, she began to think she had imagined it, only instantly there it was again, a firm, loud voice shouting "Fiona!"

Leaving the kitchen, Fiona went outside to investigate. There was not a soul in sight. She walked to the front of the house, but the garden there was also deserted. It was all very odd. Dismissing this, she went to the bottom of the garden and joined Emma in the sandpit, complimenting her on the splendid castle. Emma grinned broadly with delight and said her mommy was welcome to help. At this point there was a noise so loud and frightening both mother and daughter screamed, and Fiona grasped her daughter tight. Turning, they watched in disbelief as a large truck ploughed into the side of the house, demolishing the kitchen! A crowd gathered as if by magic and people used their cell phones to call the emergency services. All was sheer chaos and Fiona feared for the driver of the large truck.

Eventually, the driver was freed and, though he had severe injuries, the medical staff from the ambulance felt sure he would recover. The truck was eventually moved from the garden and Fiona saw that her entire kitchen was in ruins. Having been contacted, Fiona's husband arrived home from work and sat with his little girl on his lap in their neighbor's house, shaking with fright at the thought of what might have happened had his wife and daughter been in the kitchen at the time.

Some twenty-four hours later, Fiona recalled hearing the voice. At that moment, she told me, her heart literally skipped a beat. It was, after all, the voice calling her name that made her leave the kitchen and join her little girl in the garden. She knew on reflection that this was no earthly voice. "I am convinced this was my angel," she said, "and I thank God daily for the timely intervention of his messenger."

Reassurance

Angels perceive our sorrow and intervene accordingly. Many people tell me that the pain of losing a deeply loved pet can be hard to bear. Two ladies, living thousands of miles apart, wrote to me at the same time with amazing stories of angel intervention received when they were at their lowest point. Both ladies had lost a beloved dog, and life without these companions felt unbearable for them, but both believed the angels allowed the most amazing events to happen. I have received letters from every corner of the globe for some ten years now, but these stories are unique in my research. Shirley wrote to me from East Yorkshire and this is her story.

Dinky was a miniature Yorkshire terrier and so pretty that Shirley thought she looked more like a little girl than a dog! Their relationship had been close and happy for ten years, and therefore the morning Dinky took ill was most distressing. In tears, Shirley took her little dog to the vet, where sadly she died.

November, with its swirling mists, compounded Shirley's misery. Looking in despair out of the kitchen window at the gloom, she felt so low that she actually said to her husband that she would rather be dead than experience such grief. Suddenly, through the window Shirley saw the brightest light she had ever seen slowly appearing. It was so brilliant she instinctively shielded her eyes. The light shone for several seconds before slowly fading. Shirley has no doubt that this was an angel visitation, comforting her at her lowest ebb.

A few days later, while sitting in her lounge chair, Shirley was met by the most incredible sight: there appeared in front of her, as solid as before, her little dog Dinky. She was, Shirley says, exactly as when alive—literally large as life. This was not to be an isolated incident either. Dinky has appeared many times and often simply the aroma of her biscuits fill the kitchen, even though there have not been any dog biscuits in the house for years. Shirley believes that Dinky was sent to her to illustrate graphically that life is eternal and the angels ever present. She feels that she is indeed fortunate to see the proof of these facts with her own eyes.

BRONSEN

From the mist and gray of Yorkshire, we move to the heat of sunny Australia for our next story. Tracy contacted me with the story of her beloved Bronsen, a huge Rottweiler—just about as different in appearance as you could get from a Yorkshire terrier! Having no children, Tracy says that her dogs are her family. So she was distraught beyond words when Bronsen was diagnosed with incurable cancer, and could scarcely comprehend that they would only have a few short months together. The news, coming just days after a very happy Christmas, was a total blow. In March Bronsen was so very poorly that the vet had no option but to put him to sleep, after which Tracy's husband buried him in the garden. The tears flowed uncontrollably and even Tracy's other dog, Muffin, appeared to grieve.

Shortly after losing Bronsen, Tracy's husband had to leave on a business trip. He was very concerned and hated to leave

Tracy alone at such a time. There simply was not an option, however, so Tracy's husband left for five days and drove away with a heavy heart. Feeling terribly depressed, Tracy went to the garden to be near Bronsen and to pray for help and guidance. Having prayed in the past for a cure for her lovely dog, she had felt her prayers had not been answered. Now she prayed to know that Bronsen was in fact happy and whole again. Slowly and sadly, Tracy eventually made her way to bed, her little terrier Muffin by her side, and dozed into a fitful sleep.

A short time later, when it was still dark, Tracy woke, aware of a "huge thump" on the bed. Incredibly, Bronsen was bouncing on the bed with the energy of a young puppy and Muffin was joining in excitedly. Wrapping her arms around Bronsen, Tracy realized that his form was solid. A voice said to her, "Feel his throat," and following these instructions, Tracy discovered that all trace of his cancerous growths were gone. Hugging him close and stroking his ears as she had done during his life, Tracy was thrilled and overcome with happiness. Taking her hand down his chest in a long stroke, she was astonished to find that he simply vanished! There was not a gradual fading, or the sight of him jumping from the bed, or even floating away—he was gone as quickly as he had come. At this point, Tracy felt a warm, gentle hand push her back down onto the pillow and she instantly fell into a deep sleep.

The following morning, Tracy walked downstairs into her kitchen and made a cup of tea. Sitting at the kitchen table, she began to reflect on the events of the previous night. Was her mind really playing tricks on her? And yet she knew deep down that was not the case. A clear and calm voice loudly said, "Bronsen was indeed here last night." Tears flowed again, although this time they were expressions of pure happiness. Enveloped in such a strong sensation of peace, Tracy immediately understood. God had answered her prayers; her beloved Bronsen was happy and whole as in life and the angels were looking after him. She knew that one day they would be reunited in heaven.

Angels carry God's message to comfort and support. No matter what form grief may take, their unconditional love is there for all creatures great and small. The writer Ruskin summed it all up for us when he said, "To see clearly is poetry, prophecy, and religion—all in one."

guiding light insight

Angels will teach you the stillness of knowing your being is a powerful source. Angels can help you change a situation that is not of the highest good. Perception and the power are only given to those who are willing to take it to the highest level.

To invoke your angel of perception, repeat three times:

Guardian Angel of Perception, come to me.
I call upon my guide for complete perception.

WINDOW OF THE SOUL

You would be hard-pressed to find a more positive or jolly character than Irene. Twinkly and adventurous, she instantly warmed to the idea of working on stage as a medium. For many years, Irene knew she had the gift of mediumship and had been prepared to help many people in need with readings. It had been suggested that a tour of theaters, highlighting her gift for a wider audience, would be a good thing for her to do. But after her initial enthusiasm wore off, Irene began to feel rather uneasy. Was this really her "scene"? Was she intended to work in this way? Her head was saying yes, but her heart was undecided.

As the project began to take shape, she was informed that photographs would be necessary to help with publicity. A close friend who was an excellent photographer offered to take the pictures for her. One lovely bright morning they set off to the local park, with the intention of getting some atmospheric shots.

Irene's friend found the perfect location, stood Irene by a beautiful tree, and pressed the shutter. Gazing into the lens, he saw the photograph he had just taken. Not a word was said, but he looked decidedly confused. Again he had Irene pose and again pressed the shutter. In fact he did this several times, all without comment and all with a very confused expression on his face. Eventually, he passed the camera to Irene. "What can you see in the lens?" he asked.

Irene stared in disbelief. In the lens was a human eye, large, complete, and very beautiful. It was almond in shape, a greenish brown in color, and fringed with the most wonderful dark eyelashes. To say the two friends were bewildered would be an understatement. One thing was certain, however: the camera would not take photographs and the eye refused to disappear. Abandoning the session, they went home for a cup of tea and for deep reflection on what had in fact taken place.

As if by magic, it all became clear to Irene. First there was the symbolism of the third eye, indicating wisdom and insight. Second, Irene always signed her name followed by the drawing of an eye, her trademark, if you like. Third and most important, she felt this was a message, telling her that the project was not right for her, to the extent of preventing her from obtaining publicity shots. It confirmed her inner feelings and concerns, and she knew instantly that she must withdraw. Eyes are the windows of the soul and this angel eye was telling Irene to follow her soul feelings.

THE BUTTERFLY

Symbolism is a powerful way of getting messages to us, confirming that all is well with our loved ones, even though they may have left this earth, and that they love and watch over us still. This became crystal clear to Kathy, who was desperately missing her wonderful mother.

Jean, Kathy's mother, was a very special person, everyone agreed. Life had been difficult for Jean: at the age of thirty-four she had suffered from polio, which had left her handicapped.

At the age of fifty-five she was diagnosed with breast cancer. Complications from these two dreadful conditions led to her death. Kathy says it is difficult for her to find words to describe the loneliness and grief that overwhelmed her. "Jean was," says Kathy, "not only my mother but also my very best friend."

The weekend of July Fourth, Independence Day, dawned and the whole country planned celebrations and parties. Kathy, her sister, and father, however, were not in the mood to celebrate. They traveled to the family cabin in Michigan, a special place full of memories of their lovely mother. On a bright sunny morning, it was so quiet and peaceful that Kathy decided to sit on the deck and read a book. Marsha, Kathy's sister, came to join her and the sisters immersed themselves for some time in their reading.

Suddenly, the most beautiful, vibrantly colored butterfly landed on Kathy's arm. It was huge and a wonderful blue and black in hue. Incredibly still, it actually appeared to be looking at Kathy! Slowly it began to rotate on Kathy's arm and she said gently to her sister, "Look at my arm, Marsha." The butterfly seemed to be speaking to the sisters, giving them a message that it was not only beautiful but free and happy.

Marsha said at once, "You know what this means?" and Kathy replied, "Yes. God is letting us know that Mom is in heaven, beautiful, healthy, and free." Amazingly, the butterfly sat on Kathy's arm for a full thirty minutes and she felt it was such a blessing.

Several weeks later, a work colleague gave Kathy a book about the meaning of dreams. Illustrated in this book was a butterfly, blue and black in color and in fact identical to the one that had rested for such a long time on Kathy's arm. The caption under the picture read: "Butterflies are frequently used to symbolize the soul and its transformation after death." This was yet another confirmation that Kathy's mother was happy and whole again in heaven.

Working for a doctor in a very busy practice, Kathy meets lots of patients. One day, shortly after Kathy had seen the picture in the book, a lady arrived for a checkup. The tests were completed and Kathy smiled at the lady. As a child, this lady had been a neighbor; she knew Kathy and Kathy's family well. The lady returned the smile and said, "I have something for you." Intrigued, Kathy wondered what on earth it might be and watched as the lady pulled a wallet from her bag. She continued, "Forty-four years ago, your mother made this for me. I have treasured it but feel it should be yours now." Into Kathy's hand she placed a folded linen handkerchief with a beautiful blue and black butterfly embroidered in one corner! Kathy had tears streaming down her face and the lady said, "I am so sorry; it was not my intention to distress you."

"I am crying with sheer joy," said Kathy, and she told the lady about the butterfly at the cabin and in the book. "On top of all that," she told the lady, "I now have this wonderful gift, made by my mother!" The overpowering feeling was one of God showing his love and compassion and yet again confirmation that her mother was happy and well in his care.

The renowned psychiatrist Elisabeth Kübler-Ross, who died at Scottsdale, Arizona, in 2004, said her life had been profoundly changed by images of butterflies. As a relief worker she visited a Nazi concentration camp in Poland shortly after the end of the Second World War. On the barracks' walls were images of hundreds of butterflies, drawn as symbols of rebirth amidst mass deaths. It had a profound effect on her for the rest of her life.

angel affirmations

I am thankful for my life and my angel of perception.
I create perfect health for myself.
I accept wonderful experiences in my life.

ANGELIC VIBRATIONS

Cell phones are not everyone's cup of tea. Generally speaking the older we are the less we tend to use a cell phone. Teenagers, on the other hand, often appear to have cells superglued to their ears to the extent that the phones will have to be surgically removed one day. Twenty- to thirtysomethings frequently conduct business and make social arrangements via cell phones, usually on trains when I am traveling. Forty- to fifty-year-olds call to check on teenagers and arrange to take the cat to the vet. But after sixty, a cell is for an emergency only. That said, I once sat on a train watching with fascination and amusement as one eighty-plus lady sent text messages furiously for the whole journey!

Debe decided that her father really should carry a cell phone—"Just in case," she told him. In case of what exactly, she was not quite sure, but she felt much happier knowing he had one in his pocket. The only person who knew her father's number was Debe herself, but she rarely used it as it would drive him mad wondering which button to press when it rang! However, he did carry it with him as promised and Debe knew she could reach him if she needed to, and that he in turn would be able to contact her.

One day, Debe's parents spent the morning shopping, which included a visit to the jeweler's shop. Waiting to be served, they looked around the shop, noticing a large display of what could only be described as "garish" earrings. This was amusing for one special reason: Debe's father, Ralph, had been very close to his mother all her life, and she had only recently passed away at the age of 101. Ralph had loved her dearly and found her little foibles amusing. Her taste in jewelery particularly made him smile, for she would love to wear large garish costume pieces. Debe's parents looked at this display and said, "Ma"—their pet name for her—"would really love those earrings!" Chuckling, they eventually left the shop and Ralph thought what a character his mother had been and how he loved her.

Suddenly, the cell phone in his pocket started to vibrate, a pretty rare occurrence at the best of times. Ralph took the phone from his jacket pocket and started to press buttons. He seemed to have received a text message. Almost jumping out of his skin, he read the message, which said, "Love, Ma!" repeated three times. Almost unable to believe his eyes, Ralph was dumbfounded and also very moved. He had, it is fair to say, been a skeptic in these matters, but now he has no doubt that his much-loved ma had sent him a message.

All that I am, or hope to be, I owe to my angel mother.
                                    ABRAHAM LINCOLN

divine key

Perception can create the power to produce a miracle. You are ultimately in control of your life. Yours can be the greatest life, or it can be the worst. It is up to you! You can harness the power to change anything. Use this force to live in the NOW. Act on your perceptions, thoughts, feelings, vibrations, and guides. Your angel of perception gives you the permission to move forward and create your own happiness.

HEAVENLY CHIMES

As we have seen, heaven and its angels communicate in appropriate ways and through mediums we recognize. Karen's delightful story about her grandfather beautifully illustrates this fact. Harry, Karen's grandfather, had been widowed. The family worried about him, especially as he was also retired and really was a little lost. Karen's parents decided that it would be better for them all to live together and so this was arranged.

This move was not as simple as it sounds, as Karen was a tiny baby and there were several siblings in this expanding family. But a room was designated for Grandpa to allow him to have his own little haven of peace and quiet should the children be a little too exuberant! It was no surprise that Karen and her grandpa became close. He would take the little baby into his room, and she in turn offered him such comfort after losing his wife. He found a special role within the family, which pleased everyone.

Harry and granddaughter loved each other dearly. Wherever he went, Karen would go too. They shared walks, chats, stories, and a very special bond. In appearance, Harry looked like Santa—jolly, with white hair and twinkling blue eyes, full of fun. As she grew, Karen became the only child allowed in Grandpa's room, and he had upholstered a little stool for her to sit on while he told her stories. Sitting on the large mantelshelf in Grandpa's room was a wonderful chiming clock, which always seemed to chime at the appropriate part of the story! Karen loved it, and it became synonymous in her memory with Harry. The years passed, and the relationship became a joy to them both.

When Karen was just eight years old, Grandpa received word from his brother in Canada that he had been very unwell. The brothers had not seen each other for many years, and Harry decided he would take a trip to Canada and visit him. Sadly, while Harry was in Canada he suffered a series of heart attacks, and it was many months before he could come home to England. Karen positively pined for her grandpa and would go and sit in his room by herself to listen to the clock chime. The lovely familiar sound was such a comfort to her.

During this time Karen experienced a recurring dream of Grandpa getting out of a black cab, suitcase in hand, smiling. One day, the dream came true: Grandpa arrived home in a black cab, suitcase in hand, smiling broadly. Everyone was thrilled to see him home safely. When Karen was twelve years old, Harry died and she felt that she had lost her best friend as well as a grandfather. He was missed dreadfully.

Eventually, Karen married and moved into her own house, at which point she asked her mother if she could have Grandpa's clock. It took pride of place on the mantelshelf and the lovely chimes rang out once more for Karen. Imagine, then, the distress when some years later Karen's lively little boy managed to knock the clock from its position, and it was found to be irreparably broken. Nevertheless, Karen kept the lovely old time-piece and polished it lovingly, missing greatly the familiar tick and chimes.

One night, some time later, Karen found she could not sleep. Dreadfully worried about a family member who was ill, she tossed and turned with anxiety. Suddenly, the clock started to chime! In disbelief, Karen descended the stairs, but the clock was indeed happily chiming away. How on earth could that happen? Karen thought. Many clock repairers she consulted had already confirmed that it could not be mended. The family thought of a million explanations, but none turned out to be feasible. There simply was no real explanation. It was, however, the start of an amazing pattern. Whenever Karen was desperately worried about events or people in her life, the clock would start to tick and chime.

Finally, Karen realized for certain that this was her grandpa's way of being in touch, with one particular incident confirming this to be so. Karen's mother and father continued to live in the big old house where they had raised seven children and looked after Harry. As one might expect, eventually there were lots of grandchildren in the expanding family. It was simply not possible to visit each family member regularly, so it was decided that everyone would come together at the original family home instead. Consequently, the house was always full of people and laughter and the system worked very well indeed.

It was therefore virtually unheard of for Karen's parents to visit her at her own home, so it was a lovely surprise to find them coming up the path to the house one morning. Delighted, Karen opened the door. "How lovely to see you!" she beamed with delight. As Karen's mother walked through the front door and gave her daughter a hug, the clock spontaneously started to tick and loudly chimed! "Grandpa is delighted to see you here too," laughed Karen.

A Musical Bridge

We are all aware of just how comforting music can be in times of stress. Many people find music a source of solace when bereaved, or of comfort to lull them to sleep at night. It is so much a part of the fabric of our lives. I often think that a person can almost be defined by their taste in music and am fascinated to see how our musical taste can change with the passing years, as we change in life. Memories can be triggered by music, loved ones and special places evoked. So many people tell me about the importance of hearing a significant piece of music at a particular point in their life.

Singer Donna Summer tells of the time she was in Germany

and casually switched on the radio. A Barry Manilow song was on the air and the words "spirit move me" reached Donna's ears. Inexplicably, she says, a shiver ran through her and she knew the words were somehow special. Later she learned that her grandmother had died at that exact moment.

A musical link with a loved one is actually very common, although often this form of communication has to occur several times before the recipient is convinced of it. Victoria's story is confirmation of this.

Twins, most people believe, have a special empathy with each other, mentally and physically. It is common to hear of one twin suffering pain and the other twin feeling it too. For Victoria and Esther, however, nothing of the kind had ever happened. "We were close, as most sisters are," says Victoria, "but we were not aware of any special experiences of an extrasensory nature." That said, the girls shared many things as they grew up together, and their really close bond lay in their love of music. A lovely piece of music by Vivaldi called "The Four Seasons" was a particular favorite of theirs, and it could often be heard coming from the bedroom they shared in the family home.

The sisters' eighteenth-birthday celebrations were enjoyed by a large number of family and friends, wishing them well not only for their special day but for the immediate future, when both girls would be leaving home for college. Cutting the cake, the twins played "The Four Seasons" loudly, declaring that the coming autumn season would be their most exciting yet.

To Victoria's surprise, she missed her sister dreadfully at college. Having chosen schools at the opposite ends of the country, they both missed their chats and companionship hugely. Being rather shy by nature, Victoria had found it difficult to make new friends and she realized that in the past she had relied on her twin most of the time for close friendship.

Before long, the end of the girls' first term and Christmas were approaching. It was a Friday evening and all Victoria's fellow students, it seemed, had gone out to have fun. Victoria felt very lonely. Switching on the radio, she was thrilled to hear "The Four Seasons" being played and at once she felt cheered. Moments later her sister rang: she too had switched on the radio at the same moment and felt the closeness of Victoria. The girls were overjoyed; this had been the first indication of synchronicity they had experienced. Amazingly however, the wonderful coincidences continued, with the lovely music linking them several times over the following years, always at very significant times. "We both think of it as a gift from our angels," Victoria told me, "bridging the physical gap through beautiful music."

angel prayer

May the angels give me insight, wisdom, and love.
May my angels always guide me to the perfect place,
   the right place.

GOOD-BYE

It was the most beautiful Friday morning in early May. Blossoms filled the trees and the sky was that wonderful blue that lifts the spirits in early spring. Kate decided that they would eat breakfast outdoors. It would not be a long lingering breakfast, as she and her husband both had to leave soon for work, but it would be a lovely start to the day. Cereal and toast were arranged on the little patio table, and Peter smiled fondly at Kate's enthusiasm for an alfresco breakfast. "Sorry to spoil the little bit of peace," he said, "but I'm afraid that I will be home late tonight."

Kate's face fell. "I was so looking forward to a meal out and a movie," she replied. "It's been a long and busy week."

Apologizing again, Peter explained that arrangements for the conference he was organizing, which was due to start the following Monday, were nowhere near completion. But if he stayed after hours this evening, they could have the whole of Saturday together. Kate did of course understand and agreed that Saturday would be lovely; they would think of something special to do together. Kissing her good-bye, Peter left for the city.

A little while later, Kate arrived at her office and decided that she would tackle all the outstanding business that day so that she would be free to enjoy the weekend. It could get a little overpowering working for herself as a financial advisor. The hard work, however, was well worth the effort as her business was slowly growing and she felt a real sense of achievement.

Today, she told herself, I shall work right through lunch, have a sandwich at my desk, and really get the paperwork up to date.

At about 4 p.m., the phone rang and Kate sighed as she lifted the receiver, hoping it would not be a long, complicated call. To her surprise it was the hospital. Would she make her way there as quickly as possible? Her husband had suffered a heart attack. She felt as if she had turned to ice. Cold and trembling from head to foot, she grabbed the car keys as she dashed from the office.

The following days passed in a blur of grief. Peter had died before she could reach the hospital, and her mind would not accept the fact that he was gone. On the Monday morning a friend went with her to register the death. Together, they called into Kate's office to leave a message on the answering machine saying that Kate would be out of the office for the foreseeable future. As she completed all the usual formalities and dealt with the funeral arrangements on autopilot, Kate felt as if she were living someone else's life.

Some three weeks later, Kate decided that she would have to return to work. She really needed to be busy, and financially it would also be necessary. Opening the door of her little office gave her a surreal sensation; it felt like years since she was last in the little room. Behind the door lay a mountain of mail and the answering machine flashed, no doubt filled with messages. After pouring a cup of coffee for herself, Kate sat down to make a start. She pressed the Play button on the answering machine. Loud and clear the first message said, "Hello, sweetheart! Will be in touch soon—love you. Bye." It was Peter's voice.

Stunned, Kate stared at the machine. Weeks ago she had

cleared this very machine of messages when she had locked up the office. The date recorded was the day of Peter's funeral! "Impossible, I know," she says. "But I no longer look for an explanation. I just believe that this was Peter's last message, and I shall keep the tape forever."

The stories in this chapter may have helped us to open our eyes and alert our minds to the many ways angels can help us. We have seen how angels in everyday dress can appear with timely intervention in the most unexpected of situations. Even modern methods of communication can be used as a means of contact, offering confirmation that life goes on after death.

angel blessing

May the Angels bring miracles, vision, and assistance in every constructive activity with constant perfection.

~～ 6 ～

angels of
color and light

ngels, color, and light create a magical mix, with each archangel being linked to his own specific color. For example, archangel Chamuel's color is pink, and archangel Michael's color is blue. Traditionally, angels are also believed to activate with their vibrations at particular chakras. Students of yoga will be familiar with the term "chakra," which is derived from the Sanskrit word meaning "wheel." Chakras represent *prana*, which is the life force associated with centers of energy in the body. The seven key chakra points are the crown, the third eye, the throat, the heart, the solar plexus, the abdomen, and the base of the spine. In this way, Chamuel's pink activates the heart chakra, representing love, and Michael's blue activates the throat chakra, representing faith and protection.

The philosopher and mystic Emanuel Swedenborg taught that an angel's intelligence was represented by his or her color.

He said: "The garments of angels correspond to their intelligence. The garments of some glitter as with flame and those of others are resplendent as with light. Others are various colors and some white and opaque."

The following stories confirm the importance of color and angels in the lives of us all.

PINK

Special occasions are sometimes made even more so by angelic intervention and heavenly light. As we will see, angels spread light in many different forms, lifting our spirits at difficult times and spreading internal light when we feel love. The following accounts, however, feature the traditional form of light that radiates and illuminates a room.

Amy was excited and nervous in equal measures as the birth of her baby approached. Always uppermost in the mind of all parents at this point is the wish that their baby will be well. This was to be the first child in the family for both sets of grandparents—an eagerly awaited event. The pregnancy had not been without complications, and there were one or two concerns. The medical staff, however, assured Amy that such situations were not unusual and that they felt sure things would be dealt with satisfactorily.

One beautiful morning in spring, Amy knew the time was right for her to go to the hospital. Stephen, Amy's husband, carried her bag with trembling hands and off they went. The room allocated to Amy and Stephen was bright and airy, and filled with equipment. "This should cover any eventuality," Stephen remarked. All appeared to be going well until several hours later, when a doctor was called to assess the situation. The news was not good, and the complications that had been feared beforehand were now evident, so Amy would have to go to the OR.

Beside herself with fear, Amy was convinced that she was about to lose her lovely little baby and fought back the tears as she was wheeled along to the operating room. No matter how many times the nurses and the doctor said, "Don't worry; we're familiar with this type of problem. All will be well," Amy did not believe them. Shaking with panic, she silently prayed, "God and your angels, please help me!"

At this point the room and the medical staff suddenly appeared to vanish. Amy found herself surrounded by a huge, bright light and she relaxed into its soft pink warmth and glow. The sensation was simply wonderful—all her fear had gone and Amy felt content. As the light faded, she was aware of the doctor saying that they would be administering an epidural. The procedure went ahead and the baby was born, crying lustily to everyone's relief. Emma had arrived, bringing joy and happiness to the whole family. Amy was thrilled.

Later she was amazed to learn that the color pink represents love. She knew she had been surrounded by the love of angels that night.

When Emma was nine months old, the family planned a christening celebration. A little surprise was evident when Amy announced that her little daughter would be named Emma Angela. "We have never had an Angela in the family," several people remarked. "It seems an odd choice."

The little girl's parents just smiled and said, "The name is to thank the angels who attended her birth." Let them work that one out! Amy thought.

As we have seen, pink is the color attributed to archangel Chamuel, representing love and creativity. It is also the heart chakra color.

divine key

We all have the insight we need to be successful in life. You do not need to be rich to be happy, although it is important not to deny yourself or your needs. Your spiritual guidance will help you acquire and achieve whatever you need to accomplish your life purpose.

GOLD

Our second story about birth comes from Christine, who, like Amy, faced difficulties during labor. Modern technology and medical expertise are wonderful and comprehensive. Nevertheless, from time to time nature presents a challenge. It was a difficult labor for Christine; things were obviously not going smoothly and she found herself in a great deal of discomfort. Feeling utter despair and wondering just what the outcome would be, Christine felt completely helpless and overcome by sheer pain. In an instant, everything changed.

She had a sensation of running among fluffy white clouds in a clear, deep blue sky. All pain and anxiety had gone. Christine then found herself totally surrounded by a golden light, which was all enveloping and brought her such peace and love at that moment. From this instant everything proceeded as normal in her labor.

"It is a sensation I shall never forget as long as I live," Christine recalls. There have been other times in Christine's life when she has been aware of angelic influence. "I have without doubt a guardian angel," she says happily, "and a firm belief that we all have a beautiful, spiritual world to go to when this life ends."

The archangel Uriel is associated with the color gold. He represents peace and service. Gold is a color of the solar plexus.

angel blessing

O heavenly angels, I open the gates of light.
My heart sings with living water and peace.
May this light bring complete guidance into my soul.

ORANGE

The word "orange" is derived from a Sanskrit term meaning "fruitful." It was the color of the early church and of the robes for monks. In the human aura, it relates to the life force energy, and it is the color of the sacral chakra, symbolizing well-being, joy, and happiness.

Jacqueline had always felt an affinity for the color orange. She had an orange-scented oil burner that radiated peace and calm for her, and she would often take this up to her bedroom at night. On this particular evening, Jacqueline had been burning her wonderfully scented oil and had felt a lovely warm, comforting feeling as she fell into a peaceful sleep.

The following morning, she woke to an amazing sight: there, curled at the bottom of her bed was a figure. At first nebulous, it slowly formed into the shape of a woman. Although at the end of the bed, the figure was actually suspended in midair, curled into a circle and appeared to be hugging a ball-like structure. This was clearly a sight one would never expect to see on waking, but Jacqueline felt neither fear nor even surprise—it all seemed to be perfectly natural. A warm, glowing, orange light pervaded the whole scene, and sensations of glowing light and pure happiness filled Jacqueline.

Just two weeks later, Jacqueline discovered that she was pregnant. Her feelings of joy, warmth, and happiness returned in abundance. Subsequently, her little boy Jack was born, who has become a permanent source of happiness.

The events of that special morning are etched clearly in Jacqueline's mind; so much so, that as a painter, she has produced many images of the figure—a tangible reminder of the orange light of an angel.

The archangel Jophiel represents orange and yellow, and the virtues of wisdom and insight. The chakra represented is the solar plexus.

Violet

The fact that many people can conduct business from their homes has brought about one of the major changes in the world of work today. For Rob, this realization brought another bonus: not only could he work from home; he could, should he wish, relocate. The idea of leaving the big city and moving to a rural setting was very appealing to him, as his whole family would benefit from a less stressful lifestyle. The one negative aspect of all this was that it would mean moving away from Rob's widowed mother, leaving her behind in the city.

Rob's mother, Rose, however, was very supportive of the idea, urging them to follow their dream. She pointed out to them that she enjoyed a full, happy, and busy life, was perfectly healthy, and would drive her little car on frequent trips to see them. Reassured, the family made arrangements and fairly swiftly moved to a lovely rural village. It would take only an hour or so for Rose to reach them and she promised to visit often.

"Bliss" is how Rob described their new lifestyle. City traffic, noise, and pollution were things of the past. Everyone appeared to settle quickly and happily into their new life. A whole year passed and their regrets were few and far between. Even Rose enjoyed driving to the country for lovely weekends in the fresh air.

One night Rob had been working in his little office, a wooden cabin at the end of the garden, until quite late. He stood up, stretching his muscles before switching off his computer with relief. He promised himself a day off the following day after all the hours he had devoted to his business that week. Switching off the light in his garden cabin, he turned to open the door, when suddenly—to his astonishment—the cabin filled with a soft violet-colored light. Taken aback, he was baffled as to where this light could be coming from. The cabin was at the end of a long garden sheltered by trees from the house. Behind the cabin stretched fields, with no source of light whatsoever.

The light grew in intensity until Rob felt it almost enveloped him. Gradually, it faded and in bewilderment Rob closed and locked his little cabin door. It was exactly midnight when he slowly walked back to the house, still searching for an explanation.

Some time later the phone rang. It was the city hospital, which was close to where they had previously lived. In shock, Rob received the news that Rose had suffered a severe heart attack and sadly had died. Dressing quickly, he drove to the hospital to speak to the staff.

Rob was told that his mother, who had been visiting friends at the time, would have known very little about her condition. She had lost consciousness almost immediately, even though she was still alive on arrival at the hospital. "She would not have suffered," they assured him. But Rob shook uncontrollably when they explained that the registered time of death was

12 midnight! It was nevertheless a comfort to learn that even though he was not at her side, Rose had given him an angelic good-bye.

Violet, a spiritual color, has from ancient times represented mourning, and it is said to mean "you are in my thoughts." Zadkeil is the archangel of violet and represents freedom. The chakra associated with violet is the third eye and seat of the soul.

WHITE

Tara was a large, cream-colored Labrador. To say she was much loved would be an understatement—the whole household adored her, and she was decidedly spoiled. She belonged to the O'Gara family, who found the idea that she was old and failing in health difficult to cope with. Tara's favorite place was a cozy rug in front of the fire, a spot she chose to lie in more and more as she grew older, curling up to snooze. One day, the dreadful decision had to be taken to spare Tara further pain and let her go to sleep gently. John was going take Tara to the vet on the last morning while his wife, Pauline, decided that she would wait at home. Saying good-bye was hard but Pauline knew that they were doing the very best thing for Tara.

Sitting in the lounge with a cup of coffee at 8:50 a.m., Pauline gazed at the spot where Tara would normally be snoozing, wondering if in fact she had already gone to sleep for the last time. The day was dull and overcast, but all at once a bright shaft of light streamed through the window and illuminated the very spot where Tara would have lain. The light was pure white and emanated a warm feeling of love.

Sometime later John arrived home from the vet, announcing that Tara had closed her eyes and simply drifted away peacefully. "A very strange thing happened, however," John said. "Just as Tara was going to sleep, a bright shaft of light came through the window of the vet's surgery, shining directly on her."

The vet was taken by surprise, as the day was so very gray and there was no sun in the sky. "Where do you suppose that came from?" he asked. "We were both baffled," John explained.

"What time would that be?" Pauline asked.

"Well," John replied, "it was exactly 8:50 a.m., because I looked at the clock as she closed her eyes."

At that moment Pauline knew Tara had said good-bye to them both at exactly the same time. "Tara is safe in the hands of the angels," Pauline said.

White is the purest of light, representing purity, innocence, and hope. It was the color chosen by the early clergy and is an Eastern color of mourning. Gabriel has the color white attributed to him and also the qualities of hope and joy. White is the chakra color for the Higher Self.

angel meditation

Sit or lie comfortably in a dark area. Visualize yourself surrounded by a cloud of purple light energy. Open your mind and heart, and let your guardian angel of light enter your being.

Repeat silently throughout your meditation:

My heart sings with the love for my Angel of Light.

Let the angelic energy take over. When you are ready, thank your guide and let yourself surface once more to outer consciousness.

GUIDING LIGHT

When Alan was just ten years old, his family decided to leave their native Wales and begin a new life in New Zealand. Surrounded by the lovely countryside and stunning mountain scenery of New Zealand, young Alan learned to climb. He and his brothers all became keen mountaineers and loved the sport.

As Alan grew up, he was shown many photographs of his extended family and heard stories about Wales. He vowed one day to go and see this area firsthand. When he reached the age of twenty-one, he felt the time had come to do some traveling, and so he set out for Europe with a friend. High on the agenda, naturally, was a trip to Wales and Snowdonia, where the mountains attracted climbers from all over the world. Several family members still lived in the area, and Alan was very excited about meeting them and seeing the place where he had been born.

It was so thrilling to arrive at his aunt's house and meet everyone, putting faces to names and photographs. Snowdonia was a beautiful area; it reminded him of New Zealand. After a little while, he felt the urge to go climbing. Eagerly, he and his friend set out with maps and equipment for an adventure in the mountains. The views were quite stunning, and Alan felt completely at home. They really enjoyed the climbing and strenuous walks they undertook over the next two days.

Although it was early spring, the weather was very cold and a few snowflakes filled the air. Walking high in the mountains on the third day they were surprised at how quickly the weather had turned to winter once more. Thick snow and reduced light made their progress difficult. Added to this, the wind became fierce and the two young men started to feel decidedly anxious. Disoriented, they decided to make their way down the mountain as best they could. But, with virtually zero visibility, this was impossible. The young men were at a loss as to what to do next.

"Where is that guardian angel Mom is always talking about!" Alan said, only half joking.

Astonishingly, through the blizzard, they suddenly saw a light in the distance. It was very bright and illuminated what appeared to be a dwelling of some sort. Cheered by this sight, they made their way toward the light as quickly as the conditions would allow. As they came closer, they saw that the building was an old stone hut of some sort. Clearly someone was inside, so there would be shelter at least and somewhere to sit out the snowstorm in comfort.

At last they reached the old hut. On closer inspection it looked virtually derelict, but the light still shone very brightly as they approached. Knocking loudly on the door, they eagerly awaited a reply, yet none was forthcoming. The light suddenly went out and they found themselves in complete darkness once more. Hammering on the locked door several more times, Alan decided he would try to force it open. After several attempts, the door fell open inward and the two friends rushed into the hut with great relief.

It was at this point that Alan realized something very strange had happened. The hut—a single stone room in fact—was deserted, the source of light a complete mystery. Using his torch, Alan looked around and established that there was no electricity. Indeed, not even a candle that might have been burning, though the light had been so bright and powerful that no candle could possibly have produced such a glow. It was a complete mystery to be pondered upon later; for now the lads were happy to have found shelter. Snuggling into their sleeping bags, they ate the chocolate they had carried with them.

Morning dawned bright and clear. Alan was relieved to see the way down the mountain would present little difficulty now they had a clear view. Packing their things swiftly, they left the hut and made their way with ease down the mountain. Telling their story later to Alan's aunt, they told her of the complete mystery of the empty hut and bright light. First, his aunt said, "Well, Alan, we did warn you about how swiftly the weather changes up there," and second, "I believe an angel lit the hut that night, guiding you to safety." The pair fell silent, nodding intently at her explanation. Alan's friend admitted, "I can think of no other explanation, but don't you dare tell anyone I said so!"

All this took place two years ago; Alan and his friend are now safely back in New Zealand. Alan's aunt told me the story and said her nephew sincerely believes he was saved by his guardian angel. I was intrigued of course. Talking to Alan via e-mail, I asked for permission to include his story in this book. He readily agreed but added that, even to this day, his friend would not want his name used: "He would lose all credibility, he believes, as a hard climbing man of the mountains!" I could almost hear the chuckle down the line.

> There is a light that shines beyond all things
>   on Earth, beyond us all,
> Beyond the heavens, beyond the highest, the
>   very highest heavens,
> This is the light that shines in our heart.
>
> CHANDOGYA UPANISHAD

guiding light insight

Your spiritual helpers cannot do anything for you; you have to do it for yourself. Only by setting your own personal path can your spiritual guides help and support you to achieve your life dreams.

To invoke your angel of light repeat three times:

Guardian Angel of Light, come to me. I call upon my guide for complete light.

LIGHT AT THE END OF THE TUNNEL

My first impression of Bill was just how much fun he appeared to be—jolly and smiling, full of life and without a care. It had, however, been a very traumatic year indeed for Bill, as he explained, and he was still rather baffled by events.

Bill is the nickname of the Rev. William Darlison, a hardworking Unitarian minister in Dublin. In this capacity, he receives many requests for wedding services, especially in the spring and summer months. Spring 2002, however, was to prove a difficult time for brides-to-be in Bill's chapel.

Bill had seen his doctor that spring and had been given

antibiotics for an infection. As they were proving ineffective, it was clear at this point that further investigations would be required. The hospital could not offer him an appointment in less than six weeks time and maybe longer. It was all rather depressing, especially as Bill was feeling very unwell and the condition was potentially serious in nature. There did not appear to be anything he could do except wait.

One evening, Bill received a phone call from a young lady wishing to be married in his chapel. Sadly, she was told that nothing could be promised owing to the fact that Bill was still waiting for a hospital appointment, after which he might have to be admitted. "What is the problem?" the lady asked, and Bill replied it was urinary problems. The reply was rather surprising: "I am a urologist," she said. "Although I work at a different hospital from the one you're waiting to attend, I can certainly help you get an appointment quickly." Astonished, Bill thanked her, not really expecting too much, but—true to her word— she arranged an appointment only days later.

Investigations revealed cancer of the kidney that was so advanced that at first it was thought that it would be useless to begin any kind of treatment. However, a kidney was removed and further treatment initiated.

It is now eighteen months later and, as I sit and write Bill's story, he tells me that he is in remission and feels very well indeed. One thing is certain: had the lady not contacted Bill regarding her wedding that evening, and had he waited six weeks or more for an appointment, the outcome would have been very different. A wonderful, spiritual coincidence that proved to be life saving.

"What of the lady?" I asked. "Did you eventually officiate at her wedding?"

"No," came the reply, "and I do not even know her name. She simply vanished from my life."

I wondered if she had married somewhere else, or if she knew just what an angel she had been that day. For Bill, certainly, she was his light at the end of a very dark tunnel.

angel affirmations

*I accept my life in perfect harmony and
celebrate my uplifting thoughts and actions.*

*I recognize and anticipate that greatness is
always present and available for me.*

I act and speak with a pure mind.

MOONLIGHT

Nature speaks to us through sheer beauty and a simple uncomplicated spirituality that touches our hearts and souls. The power of a wonderful sunset, a rainbow, or the view from the top of a mountain can often bring us nearer to God and his angels than we are at any other time or place. At these moments, an inner voice speaks to us, as it has to mankind throughout the ages. The same sun, moon, and stars have inspired and sustained us spiritually as long as we have been on this earth. In our next story, Matthew explains how he feels the angels spoke to him one clear moonlit night long ago and changed his life forever.

Walking alone down the central aisle of the long greenhouse, Matthew touched the leaves of the plants, bent his head to smell the fragrance, and occasionally plucked a dead leaf from a flower. It was late evening and for Matthew the best time of the day. All the customers and visitors had left his little garden center, and he was able to wander around in peace and contentment.

Ever since he was a small boy, he felt himself drawn to plants and gardening. He would join his grandfather in his extensive kitchen garden, and be thoroughly absorbed in everything he saw and touched. His parents were a little bemused that a child so young should have a passion for gardening but felt it was a good hobby to grow up with. Both Matthew's parents were doctors, and it was presumed that he too would have a career in medicine.

The years passed and Matthew discovered that he was less academic by nature and inclination than his parents. He had to work extremely hard at school simply to keep up. Private tutors were hired to boost his learning capacity, and he scraped by with just enough qualifications to get him into a university to study medicine. His parents were thrilled but Matthew grew increasingly despondent. He had virtually no interest or aptitude for medicine and found himself embarking on the course only to make his parents happy. How he hated his first term—he felt inadequate and totally miserable. He was quite at a loss as to what to do next. Sleep was a problem for him owing to his anxiety, and he had several migraine attacks as the weeks went by. It was a few days before he would be returning home for the first break of the academic year, but Matthew dreaded going home and confessing his unhappiness. It was a difficult dilemma.

The night before the end of the term, Matthew found it impossible to sleep as usual. At midnight he got out of bed to go for a walk around the college grounds. It was a rather cold and crisp night, but that suited his mood. Walking slowly, he turned a corner and was suddenly confronted by the most wonderful full moon in the dark sky. It was so very bright and beautiful, it took Matthew's breath away. The whole scene was illuminated and he felt his heart lift. Stunning white clouds drifted slowly across the sky and the whole atmosphere was quite magical. Suddenly, as Matthew stared upward, a white cloud appeared to be taking shape before his eyes: it was a huge angel! This angel cloud was perfect in every detail—head, wings, flowing robe—and totally surrounded by the silver light from the moon. It filled Matthew with a sensation that he could not articulate. In an instant, however, he knew exactly what he must do and he made a life-changing decision on the spot.

Arriving home, he asked his parents to sit down and listen to what he had to say about his future. Pouring out his heart, he told them how medicine was not for him and that he wanted desperately to be a gardener. It was rather a shock, as you can imagine, for the confused parents, but they loved him and wanted him to be happy. It was patently obvious that he must leave his course and follow his heart.

Many years later, here he is happy and content, walking along the path of his long, plant-filled greenhouse. The garden center, though small, is very successful, and all because Matthew had taken a stroll by moonlight and found an angel.

Matthew is extremely fortunate to know exactly what he
wants to achieve in life and to be thoroughly content in his chosen path. He is passing on his love and enthusiasm for nature
and the natural world, spreading beauty to all around. His happiness and good fortune bring to mind the following blessing
by the Rev. Beryl Allerton:

If you have found friendship, then be a friend.
If you have found peace, go in peace.
If you have found comfort, be a comforter.
If you have found love, take it as a light for the world.

HEAVENLY LIGHT

This is my story: it happened very recently and certainly
brought light into my life. In order to understand the story,
I shall have to give you a little background information. As a
child I was fortunate enough to live in a close community with
an extended family and wonderfully friendly neighbors. One of
my neighbors had two daughters who were the same age was,
and so I would spend a great deal of time in their home. The
mother of this family was called Ethel. She was very sweet,
though a little shy and with a tendency to be rather serious.
Almost subconsciously, I would try to make Ethel laugh, usually
by making fun of her hats! She took all this teasing on board in
a delighted fashion and would tell me, "You're a rum one!"—
an expression common to the North of England, meaning that
she thought I was a funny girl. Making Ethel giggle certainly

made me happy, and she was very much a part of my childhood. In my early teens, the neighborhood families became scattered and my immediate family moved a considerable distance from Ethel, so sadly I never saw her again.

Forty years passed. Then, one day, I was invited to visit an alternative health center in North Manchester. The owner, Joan Evans, had invited several people who wished me to sign my books for them and to listen to their stories for my research. A warm, spiritual atmosphere pervades this center, owing in part to Joan, a delightful, kind, and spiritual lady. Driving along, I passed the crematorium where I knew Ethel had been cremated only a few years before. I started to think about her and explained to my husband how much fun we had in that community and how Ethel would teasingly scold me. I spoke of Ethel all the way to the center.

It was a lovely afternoon spent meeting people, listening to their stories, and signing books, and generally talking about angels. The center also has a resident medium, although I was not aware of this fact. His name is Sean Lucas, and he's a pleasant, unassuming young man. Toward the end of the afternoon, he asked me if he could have a word in private so Joan indicated that we could use her office. Closing the door, Sean said to me, "I hope I am not frightening you in any way, but when you came through the door today, a lady in spirit came with you." A little baffled, I said I was not at all concerned. He continued, saying, "The lady is still with you, smiling broadly. She says her name is Ethel!" I was, to say the least, surprised but thrilled at the news. Sean then said, "The message continues, 'I used to call her rum!'" I was now astonished, especially as Sean went on to tell me many facts about Ethel, including her very unusual maiden name. He ended the message by telling me, "Ethel says that she is very happy and laughs a lot. She is watching over you and sends her love."

I feel so blessed to have Ethel sending love and light from heaven.

divine key

Our thoughts determine the activity of our lives; thoughts are things and manifest after their kind. It is not enough to know these principles or to connect with angelic beings—we must demonstrate them in our daily affairs.

LIGHT AS A FEATHER

Forgive the angelic pun above, but I feel that it is not only appropriate in relation to the following story but also for many people such simple symbolism—light and feathers—proves to be the most illuminating experience of their lives.

It was already dark and the temperature was dropping sharply as Mary stepped into the busy city street. Tightening her scarf around her neck, with thoughts of home she made her way to the parking lot. What a week it had been, she thought, with six long days spent under intense pressure preparing for a very important seminar. Saturday evening had arrived at last. The seminar had been a huge success and all her hard work had paid off. But it was still difficult to relax, as her stress levels had been so high for so long.

Smiling to herself, she thought of the warmth and the smell of a roast cooking as she entered the house. Her partner had been given instructions as to when the roast should be put into the oven and the vegetables prepared. It would be lovely to sit down with the family before driving her son to his venue for Saturday night socializing. Maybe I'll treat myself to a little drink while waiting for the vegetables to cook, she thought. I shall really unwind then. Leaving the city with a sigh, Mary calculated that in only about half an hour she would be home.

Turning the key in the lock, Mary was astonished to find the house in darkness. Not only was there plainly no one else at home but there was no smell of a welcoming roast! The meat—cold as the day itself—sat on the kitchen table. At this point, it was the last straw. Fighting back the tears, Mary took off her coat and began to prepare the meal, wondering where on earth her partner and son could possibly be. She felt her stress levels shooting up again.

Placing the roast in the oven and setting the table, she decided that the only thing she could think of to soothe her was to do a little ironing. Ironing may be a task hated by many, but it never ceased to calm Mary and she could think more clearly as she worked. As she began to iron, she realized that her stress was compounded by the fact that she no longer had her mother to confide in when things were difficult.

Six months previously, while on holiday, Mary had received a phone call that had turned her life upside down. Her mother had died unexpectedly yet peacefully while sitting in her favorite chair. It was nevertheless beyond comprehension—only days before Mary had waved good-bye, and her mother had cheerfully wished them a lovely holiday. She had shown no sign whatsoever of ill health. The bond of mother and daughter can often be a comfort and a blessing, and they had been so very close. Now here she was, six months later, wishing she could phone her mother and tell her all the troubles of the day. How she missed her! Hot tears stung her eyes, as she tried to iron away her anxiety.

The ironing done, she put away the board and opened the door of the little laundry room that led into the kitchen. There, in the middle of the kitchen floor, was a large white feather! Yet no one had entered or exited the kitchen while Mary had been ironing and the house was still empty save for her. All the windows and doors were shut to keep out the cold, and the feather certainly had not been there before Mary stepped into the laundry room.

Shaking with emotion, Mary realized the implication of this amazing sight and her tears began to flow in earnest. But how on earth was she going to explain to her family what made her cry? If they suddenly arrived home, they would certainly find it difficult to believe that she had burst into tears because the roast was not in the oven!

We chatted about the feather shortly after this incident. Mary was convinced that it had been a gift from an angel—an angel who was her mother, no less. I agreed. Ten months have passed and Mary continues to receive feathers at specific moments whenever she needs support and comfort. There have also been moments of joy when her mother seems to be signifying that she is especially close. These include special occasions such as when her much-loved grandson received his college degree. This comes as a joy and a comfort for Mary, with the feathers shedding light on her belief that we are never alone.

THE LIGHT INSIDE

The words "open heart surgery" would strike fear into the bravest of mortals. Christine says that she was so terrified the night before her visit to the operating room that she begged her husband to take her home. Trembling, she told him that she simply could not face such extensive surgery and wished to take her chances without it. Her husband tried his best to calm her, but it was getting late and he was told by the nursing staff that he had to go, much as he hated leaving Christine in such a distressed state.

Glancing across to the bed opposite her own, Christine was suddenly aware that the lady occupying that bed was crying bitterly, and so it was not long before Christine was crying too! Both ladies were facing the same operation and struggling with their nerves.

After a little while, Christine had calmed a little and realized that she must do the only thing possible in her situation: pray. The act of asking God for help with her fright and to send her comfort helped to lift Christine's tearful mood a little. She also recalled that her grandmother had been a nurse in this very hospital many years before. Although her grandmother had died when Christine was only twelve years old, she treasured her loving memories of such a kind lady. Now Christine entreated her to send angelic help.

Almost instantly, a warm glow spread from the top of Christine's head all the way to her toes. It was the most wonderful sensation and, as the feeling subsided, so did her fear. Calm and confidence surrounded Christine and she realized instinctively all would be well. Knowing how upset her husband had been when leaving her, Christine phoned to tell him she was now fine and that he must not worry. Completing the call, Christine was astonished to hear a voice telling her that her fellow patient would also be perfectly fine: both operations would be successful. Completely relaxed by now, Christine climbed into bed and fell into a deep refreshing sleep.

Morning dawned and Christine woke. To her amazement she was still calm and confident, facing her surgery with the firm belief that her prayers had been answered. As predicted, both ladies had successful operations and have gone on to lead happy lives, putting all their fears behind them. However, one thing Christine will never forget is the lovely glow from the angels that calmed her so in her darkest hour.

angel prayer

May the light of angels surround me,
The love of angels enfold me,
The power of angels protect me.

May the angels always watch over me.

THE EVERLASTING LIGHT

The angels have always been very close to Heather and she has needed them more than most. A young wife and the mother of five-year-old Jason, Heather felt that her world had been turned upside down, never to be the same again, when she received the devastating news that her husband, Paul, was suffering from terminal cancer. So many emotions and thoughts encompassed Heather, raising painful questions about the future. Her greatest concern, however, was for Paul. There were three aspects of this awful journey they were all embarking on that gave rise to particular concern for Heather. First, she wanted Paul to die at home, and on a Sunday, which felt special and is a day of peace. Second, she desperately wished to be with him when the moment came, yet hoped that Jason would be spared the experience. The third worry for Heather was the actual manner

139

of Paul's death. She desperately wanted this to be gentle and pain free, allowing him to transcend to the next world with ease. Sitting alone, Heather expressed these desires to a higher source, uncertain as to what exactly that source might be.

Inevitably the day came when Paul had to leave his little family, and all of Heather's concerns were met. Heather was indeed with Paul as he died, but Jason was out of the house. This eased the burden of loss a little.

Immediately before Paul died, Heather had asked him if there was any way that he could let her know that he was well and happy in the next life. One week later, Heather was standing in her kitchen, thinking about her husband and hoping that all was well with him wherever he might be. Suddenly, such a strong tingling sensation ran down her spine that instinctively she turned around. There stood Paul. It was the most wonderful moment—yet there was such an air of normality about it. Paul was wearing a blue sweatshirt familiar to Heather, but he had, she says, "a silver sparkle completely surrounding him." He told Heather that all was well, that she must not worry, and then he quickly vanished.

Incredibly, some time later, Paul appeared once more. This time Heather sensed a huge difference in Paul: he had wings and glowed with a sense of knowledge, as if he had discovered the answers to everything and had ascended to a higher state.

Years have passed and Heather has had many indications that the angels are helping her. Spiritual experiences in the form of a beautiful voice, warm tingling sensations, and feelings of pure love convince Heather that she has her very own guardian angel. The knowledge that Paul is now an angel, combined with the powerful sensation that the two of them are still connected, assures Heather that the bond of love can never be erased—not even by death.

angel blessing

May the angels activate our Inner Light,
and create miracles around us at all times.

Pure white light, of course, contains all the colors of the rainbow, and angels, as these stories have suggested, appear in every hue. White light, which appears to so many people, signifies many angels reaching out to us with love. The whole beautiful spectacle is summed up in the following quotation:

There appeared to me very beautiful rainbows, as on former
occasions, but still more beautiful, with a light of the purest
white, in the center of which was an obscure, earthly something:
but that most lucid snow-white appearance was beautifully var-
ied by another lucidity . . . and, if I rightly recollect, with flow-
ers of different colors round about.

EMANUEL SWEDENBORG

When related to angels, love and light are synonymous. Angelic love can help us to make decisions, heal our fears, and comfort us in so many ways. As the stories in this chapter illustrate, the type of light and color of light that accompany angels are highly significant and personal to each individual and that person's specific needs. We all have this special light within us, and exercising this light will enable us to spread love to others. If we were all to practice radiating light and love, who knows how it could spread throughout this troubled world!

~ 7 ~

angels of love

Angels nourish us by continually sending us a steady flow of love. Allow yourself to feel their love, to step into it, accept it, and be with it in this perfect moment. If you choose to welcome angelic love into your life, it will raise your spirit up to the heavens.

LOVE IN THE FACE OF ADVERSITY

Some people are plucky, some are brave, and a rare few are heroes. Mark Thallander definitely belongs in the last category. His story is humbling and inspiring in equal measures, and may make you earnestly count your blessings.

It began one evening when Mark was driving to the house of his friend Gary de Vaul to share a family dinner. A close friend of Gary and his family for many years, Mark was looking forward to the evening immensely. As a hugely successful organist, Mark had recently given concerts in Carnegie Hall and St. Patrick's Cathedral in New York. This evening it would be lovely to relax and chat about the concerts with his close friends over a meal.

With dinner more than ready, Gary and his wife expressed surprise at Mark's absence. Usually a very punctual person, Mark could be relied on to arrive exactly on time. Trying in vain to think of an explanation, they could do nothing but wait and hope their dinner would not spoil.

The date was August 3, 2003, and summer storms dogged Mark as he drove to Gary's house in Maine. When exiting the turnpike just minutes from his destination, Mark's car hydro-planed. After the accident, he recalls a strange silence and then hearing a lovely, calming woman's voice giving him instruc-tions and urging him to keep his eyes open, thereby preventing his slide into unconsciousness and in effect saving his life.

The silence was shattered by the sound of fire trucks and ambulances arriving with sirens wailing. The paramedics who took care of him on the ride to the hospital could see immedi-ately how serious this accident was: Mark had severed his arm in three different places. On reaching hospital, it became clear that Mark would lose his left arm. "Please save my arm," he asked repeatedly. "I am an organist."

Having received the terrible news of his friend's accident, Gary arrived at the hospital. He recalls that Mark amazingly never lost his sense of humor and was cracking jokes, even at this darkest of times! The prospect of serious surgery after such a severe loss of blood was extremely dangerous; however,

Mark had thousands of people praying for him. The surgeons saved his life but nevertheless there would be a long road ahead toward recuperation.

Therapy followed the operation, and Mark literally had to learn to walk again as losing an arm severely alters the body's balance. Just four short months later, Mark returned to his home church of Lake Avenue, Pasadena. He sat before the church's behemoth organ and played a duet with a fellow organist for an audience of several hundred. He has since worked at condensing scores and increasing the role of his right hand. But his determination to play ever more complicated music with the aid of a mechanical arm is further testament to this remarkable man's courage.

One special fact emerged as Mark recovered. The authorities told Mark that there was no record of a woman at the scene when they arrived, even though a calming female voice had kept him alive. Mark is therefore convinced that he heard the voice of an angel. "God let me live for a purpose," he says. "Maybe I can inspire others to fulfill their dreams." Inspire he certainly does, and he is living proof of the power of love. His family and friends clearly loved him, but the love of God and his angel also saved this very special man.

> Did the star   wheels and angel wings,
> with their holy winnowings
> Keep beside you all the way?

> ELIZABETH BARRETT BROWNING

angel blessing

O heavenly angels, I open the gates of love.
My heart sings with living water and peace.
May this love bring complete balance and fulfillment to my soul.

angel meditation

Sit or lie comfortably in a dark area. Visualize yourself surrounded by a cloud of purple light energy. Open your mind and heart, and let your guardian angel of love enter.

Repeat throughout your meditation:

My heart sings with love for my Angel of Love.

Let the angelic energy take over your being. When you are ready, thank your guide and let yourself surface to the outer consciousness.

WEDDING DAY ANGEL

Grandmothers and their grandchildren often share a very special bond. This is especially true when they live together in the same house. Certainly this was the case with Emma, who had lived with her grandmother from the very tender age of eleven months. Emma's family lives in the beautiful town of Llandudno in North Wales, a very spiritual part of the British Isles. The wonderful seascapes and the backdrop of the mountains give this area a very special atmosphere.

Llandudno is, of course, a Welsh-speaking part of Wales, so Emma grew up calling her grandmother "Nain," which is Welsh for "grandmother." Their relationship was very close and special, so Emma felt blessed growing up in a home surrounded by love. But, sadly, her Nain, who for some time had been suffering with motor neurone disease, died when Emma was twenty years old. Nain was missed dreadfully by the whole family, especially by Emma.

Seven years passed and in the late summer of 2004, Emma was to be married. Her mother, Gwen, told me that everything was in place and the day dawned with sunshine and happiness. The only cloud in the sky for Emma was the fact that her much loved Nain would not be there to see her walk down the aisle. One morning some time earlier, when Gwen and her friend Pauline had been drinking coffee while discussing the wedding arrangements, Emma announced that she had a plan. On her wedding day, she would call at the cemetery on her way to the church and show Nain her wedding dress, feeling sure her spirit would be watching over her on this special day. Pauline laughed and said, "Your Nain will not be hanging around the cemetery on such a day; she will be with you—wherever you are!" They all laughed and agreed that it made sense that Nain would be watching over Emma on her wedding day of all days.

Well, here they were on Emma's big day, about to get ready for the lovely occasion. Emma told Gwen that she wished to get dressed in Nain's bedroom, as this would help her to feel close to her. Nain had also died in the room, and Emma always remembered her Nain being there. Gwen watched with pride as Emma put on the beautiful wedding gown, headpiece, and the traditional garter for luck. She looked so beautiful and happy; it was a treasured moment.

Suddenly through the window floated a pure white feather. The window was only slightly open, and sloping outward, making it difficult for a feather to enter, to say the least. Yet the feather drifted directly toward Emma, settling at her feet. Bending to pick it up, Emma said, "Nain is here and I am going to take her to church with me." She placed the feather in her garter, happy in the knowledge that her day was complete. It really would be the happiest day of her life.

It was wonderful to hear that Emma recognized the symbolism of the feather instantly, confident in the knowledge that this was from her grandmother. So many of us receive symbols from departed loved ones, especially feathers, yet find it difficult to believe in them. Such people often ask me if I believe that they have received a sign, and it is always lovely to see their faces light up when they realize that many others like them have been given symbols at difficult or significant times in their lives. For the second time, while writing this book, I am reminded of words from Psalm 91: "He shall cover thee with his feathers, and under his wings shalt thou trust."

GRANDMA'S LOVE

We are all familiar with the expression "the terrible twos," but Lesley says her little girl, Beth, also went through the terrible threes, the horrible fours, and was still causing havoc through year five! Many nights found Lesley and her husband at their wit's end as they tried to get Beth to go to bed without a fight—often to no avail.

One particularly difficult week, Lesley had driven daily to see her mother, who was very ill. This, combined with Beth's bad behavior at home, was simply wearing her out. Lesley was tired, worried, and mentally exhausted, and the behavior of her little daughter was simply the last straw. "I love her so much," Lesley told me, "but I could not cope at that time at all!"

One evening that week, just as the nightly battle for bed was about to commence, Lesley received a phone call from her sister to say that their mother had been taken to the hospital and was seriously ill. Leaving her husband with the screaming Beth, Lesley drove to the hospital in tears. Holding her mother's hand, Lesley and her sister had time to tell her how much they loved her and to say their good-byes. Gently their mother slipped away, to join their father in heaven, said Lesley. It was a long night and naturally no one could sleep. Back at home, Lesley and her husband sat up most of the night, drinking tea and talking about her mother and the lovely person she had been. The one consolation was that her mother had not suffered a long lingering illness; it had been pretty quick, which they all agreed was a blessing.

Morning came and Beth appeared in her pajamas, looking angelic and smiling broadly at her weary parents. The day progressed and Beth was as good as gold. "Thank heaven for small mercies," Lesley said to herself. After dinner, Beth chose her bedtime story and her father read to her before gathering her up in his arms to carry her to bed. Lesley braced herself for the battle. To her parents' astonishment, Beth went through her entire bedtime routine without a single moment's hesitation or complaint. Completely unaided, she climbed into bed and asked for a good-night kiss. Lesley and her husband bent to hug the little girl and gave her a kiss saying, "What a very good girl you have been tonight!"

Imagine their surprise when Beth replied, "I promised Grandma I would be good."

"When was that, darling?" Lesley asked.

"This morning," Beth replied. "She was sitting on my bed when I woke up and said she loved me, and wanted me to be a good girl for Mommy and Daddy!"

Not only did this dramatic improvement in Beth's behavior make a very sad time a little easier, but it eased Lesley's mind to know that her much-loved mother was watching over them.

Angels descending, bringing from above,
Echoes of mercy, whispers of love.

FANNY J. CROSBY

guiding light insight

If we accept love into our lives we will have the opportunity to stand in our own truth and authenticity. When we leave the present moment of love for a maze of "if onlys" or "what ifs," we move into an area of insecurity. By loving and accepting love, we get to stand in the love and security of our true self.

To invoke your angel of love, repeat three times:

Guardian Angel of Love, come to me. I call upon my guide for complete love.

MAXINE'S ANGEL

Babies arrive whenever they feel the time is right for them to enter the world, which is frequently at a most inconvenient moment for the mother! Maxine's little girl, Megan, was celebrating her second birthday and great excitement filled the air. Maxine was extremely busy with a room full of two-year-olds demanding drinks and goodies to eat. Feeling tired owing to the fact that it would be only three weeks until her next baby was due, Maxine nevertheless wanted this to be a special day for her little girl. Suddenly, a rather familiar pain interrupted her thoughts of candle lighting, and Maxine said silently, "No, it can't be now—I'm too busy!" The pain became more insistent and when Maxine's mother arrived to help with the party, she assessed the situation rapidly, telling her daughter that it was "time to go." Trying to stay calm and controlled, they lit the birthday candles, sang "Happy Birthday," and, leaving other mothers in charge, made a dash for the car. Just as they opened the door to leave, Maxine's husband arrived home and was promptly pushed back outside to accompany them to hospital.

Maxine's one clear memory of that car dash was the strange fact that a large, bright light shone directly in front of the car all the way to the hospital. It was by now very dark, the middle of January, and the light—brighter than any headlights yet without any apparent source—illuminated the way. There was little time to waste on arrival although at first the staff seemed rather slow, as they were initially unaware of the urgency.

Soon, however, they rushed Maxine to the delivery room, when it became clear that time was running out, so to speak. Maxine felt strongly that something was seriously wrong. She was in great pain and experienced rising panic. Silently she began to pray for help. Instantly she felt the most amazing sensation of comfort, love, and warmth. All pain vanished as Maxine seemed to leave her body, floating upward in a typical out-of-body experience. A calm voice told her to relax, that all would be well.

At that moment, Maxine heard her mother's voice say clearly, "You have another baby girl!" Her return to her body at astonishing speed was the only part of the whole experience that Maxine found frightening. Seeing her mother's face, full of concern, Maxine tried to explain, but her mother told her to relax and look at her lovely baby, born on the same date as little Megan.

As Maxine was wheeled into a ward with other new mothers, the nurse said to her, "Go to sleep now and you will feel better in the morning." But even though Maxine was exhausted, she simply could not sleep as the dramatic events of the day were still whirling around her head. She quietly thanked God for the safe delivery of her little girl.

Early the next morning, at about 7 a.m., the nurse came into the ward and said to Maxine, "Your mother is on the telephone. Would you like to speak to her?" The voice on the other end of the telephone was not only worried but approaching panic: "Maxine, are you alright?" Maxine assured her mother that she was fine and asked why she was so distressed.

"Waking this morning," her mother explained, "I was astonished to see a huge angel standing at the foot of my bed. Truly awesome, it must have been at least eight feet tall. I knew the angel was connected with you, and of course for a moment I feared the worst. As I grabbed the phone to dial the hospital, this amazing creature floated above my head and I could see how massive the figure was." The angel had a wingspan of approximately thirteen feet and robes containing every color of the rainbow: it must have been an awesome sight indeed.

On reflection, Maxine's mother realized this was a positive message saying that all was well, not a fearful image at all. Later that same day, Maxine told her mother of her own wonderful experience at the point of delivery. With great wisdom, her mother said they should not question these incredible events but thank God for all his blessings.

angel affirmations

❦

I radiate constant love and abundance.
I believe in the power of love.
I give thanks for my angel of love.

THROUGH THE EYES OF A CHILD

Whenever people tell me of their childhood angelic experiences, they always add that these events have remained crystal clear in their memory. All other childhood memories may fade or be hazy, but those of angelic encounters remain as vivid as if they had happened only today. Sue told me that she can recall her experience instantly, almost as though she were replaying a tape of the events in her mind's eye. The wonderful experience has been a comfort all her life.

Living in the North of England as a young girl of ten, she was aware of how ill her father was. Family illness represents a particularly difficult time for any youngster, as often their stress and worry may not be evident to the rest of the family, who may believe that the child is coping well.

One night, Sue was asleep in her bed. Something, and it

is difficult to know what exactly, wakened her. The whole of Sue's bedroom was flooded with light, which astonishingly did not hurt her eyes at all. The light was particularly surprising given that Sue had been in a deep sleep only seconds earlier. When she opened her eyes, Sue was facing the wall but she felt a strong compulsion to turn around and sit up in bed. It was then she saw the angel.

The details and the sensations of this amazing sight are etched firmly in her memory, and Sue had no trouble describing them to me. "It was hard to assign a gender to this figure," she said. "It appeared completely androgynous." By contrast, the outline of the angel's features were distinct, and so Sue concentrated on them, determined to take in every detail. She noted the folded wings of the being and the details of its abundant hair.

No trace of fear or apprehension of any kind affected Sue. She explains, "My only concern was to get a really good look at this wonderful angel." The light and with it the angel slowly started to fade. Calmly, ten-year-old Sue lay down again in her bed and promptly went to sleep! This is something that also appears to be very typical of people who have an angelic experience: because of the amazing nature of the event, they are somehow instructed to sleep again immediately—an obvious coping mechanism.

Shortly after the angel's visit, Sue's father died. It would appear that the angel was sending a comforting message to the little girl; it seemed to be saying that angels would take good care of her father and that heaven was indeed very close. Throughout her life, Sue has been aware that she is not alone, the angels are close and she has that wonderful fact to sustain her.

LUCY'S ANGEL

Lucy was only six years old when she was admitted to the hospital with a mysterious illness. Tests were under way, but Lucy was doing very poorly indeed and Karen, her mother, was white-faced with worry. Karen's husband was away on business and she was having trouble contacting him. Holding Lucy's hand, she prayed all would be well with her lovely daughter. Slowly, during the course of the day, Lucy's condition did appear to be improving and the medical staff kept a close eye on her.

Early in the evening, Karen went to try to phone her husband again and also to collect a much-needed cup of tea. On her return to Lucy's bedside, she was surprised to see her little daughter smiling broadly. "Are you feeling much better darling?" Karen asked, delighted.

"Yes, Mommy!" Lucy replied. "Grandma made me laugh. Did you bring her a cup of tea?" Lucy looked at an empty chair on the other side of the bed and chuckled. Karen hugged her daughter, relieved that she was so much improved but feeling confused.

"Mommy, she's gone—you missed her," Lucy exclaimed. "She had such a lovely silver dress."

At once Karen understood and she said aloud, "Thank you, Mom!" It was almost a year since Karen's mother had died, but shaking with emotion Karen realized that she had taken care of her little granddaughter.

This is yet another story that illustrates just how close

grandparents can be to their much-loved grandchildren, and how they remain close and protective even after death.

divine key

Our desire and need for love is so deep that we find ourselves constantly searching for love. We look for it in people, material things, food, and even animals. The turning point in your journey will come when you know you don't need love—you *are* love. You are then truly open to giving and receiving love.

ALL-EMBRACING LOVE

A person experiencing an angelic encounter will often struggle for words to describe their experience. The English language simply fails them at such times—the whole event is so unique that it positively defies description. There can be no doubt, however, as to the effect their amazing experience usually has on the lives of the individuals concerned. This was certainly the case with Dawn. She was lost for words when she tried to describe the love she felt when she met an angel.

A young, busy mother, Dawn was struggling with severe personal problems and grief. The days seemed to blend seamlessly and yet Dawn's situation was not getting any easier. Her emotions intensified almost imperceptibly, until everything simply became too much for her. Dawn began to cry as if her heart would break, and she was unable to stop the flow of her tears. All day long she sobbed, only managing to control herself slightly when putting the children to bed. An emotional tide of grief washed over her, and Dawn realized she had reached an all-time low. It was still early in the evening but Dawn just wanted to lie down in bed and be alone. Drawing the curtains against the light of the evening, she climbed into bed.

Sleep is not very likely, she told herself, but her exhaustion was such that she had to rest. A calm came over her and she relaxed. Looking up at the ceiling, her eye was drawn to a series of small sparkling golden lights. A shadow on the ceiling also was perplexing. The curtains were drawn, but it was too light outside to cast shadows. What on earth could it be? Dawn had no idea. Maybe it's because my eyes are so very sore from constant crying, she reasoned. Perhaps the lights are coming from within like a migraine? Leaving the bed she walked to the window. Outside, all appeared normal. There was no explanation for twinkling lights out there. It was all a puzzle and so Dawn climbed back into bed, still gazing at the shadow and lights on the ceiling.

At this point, there was a huge flash of light. Dawn sat bolt upright with surprise but nothing could have prepared her for the sight that then met her eyes. The room was full of angels, flowing in and out of her line of vision. It was truly awesome. Dawn felt no fear or anxiety of any kind; in fact her feelings of happiness were overwhelming.

Suddenly, one angel detached itself from the group and flew down directly in front of Dawn's face. Her appearance was almost magical. Young, very beautiful, and dressed in virtually white light, she had small, fragile wings. Her hair was glowing and streaming back from her face as though wind-swept. Slowly, the angel reached forward and touched Dawn's face. This is the moment when Dawn struggles to find words to describe the sensations. The love, she says, was so pure. It was an all-enveloping kind of love she had never known before, making this a moment she will hold dear for life.

As Dawn sat transfixed, myriad angels continued to flow around the room as if heaven had momentarily come down to earth. Slowly and gently, the vision began to fade until the last angel had gone. Once more the ceiling was a normal white and the room appeared as usual. Dawn, however, would never be the same again! She told me that the feeling had been one of being wrapped in cotton wool, loved, and protected, and knowing that she would never feel so alone again. The following day, Dawn was possessed with energy unlike any she had ever experienced in her life. Now she has hope for the future and a constant sense of all-embracing love.

angel prayer

May the Angel of love surround me with trust.
May the oceans bless me with light and divine purpose.
I celebrate life's beauty, in all its joy and love.

AN ANGEL FOREVER

Grandma was the glue, the loving bond that kept the whole family together. A jolly, witty, and fun-loving matriarch, she was adored by all who knew her. Ever since she was a little girl, Paula had called this lovely lady Nana. Nana was Paula's grandmother and best friend. No matter how dark things appeared, Nana would make Paula laugh and the little girl loved her unconditionally.

Young at heart, Nana looked years younger than her actual age; her lively mind was interested in everything and everyone. A bookseller by trade, she attracted many people to her business, many of whom came simply for the pleasure of talking to her. Without a shadow of doubt, Nana was a colorful character who seemed larger than life. Indeed, so much so that no one could ever imagine life without her.

Paula was heartbroken and inconsolable when Nana died. Nana's short illness took everyone by surprise as normally she was so healthy. To Paula's great distress, Nana died before she had the chance to say good-bye to her or to tell her one more time how much she loved her. Yet amazingly, and with some consolation to Paula, Nana died as she had lived, with a smile on her face. The family members who had been by her bedside reported that Nana appeared to have seen her husband, who had died some years earlier. She said, "I can see Granddad, he is smiling" and shortly afterward, she peacefully slipped away to join him.

Immediately after the funeral, Paula was at her lowest ebb. Not only was she missing her much-loved Nana terribly, but other personal problems piled on top of her grief, leaving her feeling emotionally and physically drained. One evening, overcome with it all, she sat alone in her house. Wishing to find some inner peace, she lit a scented candle and tried to meditate. Memories flooded her mind as the lovely blue flame gently flickered on her mantelpiece. Exhausted, she quickly fell asleep.

Waking with a start, Paula was aware of a strange crackling noise and found to her horror that the candle had set fire to a card on the mantelpiece, which in turn had ignited the wallpaper! Dashing in panic to the kitchen, she returned with a bowl of water to throw over the wall. Mercifully, this was sufficient to extinguish the flames but she shook with the thought of what might have happened. Recalling how tired she had been, having not slept properly for days owing to the pressure of grief and problems, she had fallen into a very deep sleep. But what was the strange noise that had woken her and in effect saved her life? She was mystified.

Wearily, Paula made her way up to the bedroom, feeling fortunate but very alone in her sorrow. As she entered her bedroom, her CD player, which had been broken these past few months, switched itself on, flooding the room with the most ethereal music. Delicate harps played, enveloping and lifting Paula's spirit. As she listened in wonder, a voice, strong and familiar, spoke to her. It was Nana: "I love you, Paula," she said.

Paula will never forget that wonderful moment and says that, without a doubt, she has an angel forever.

angel blessing

May the blessings of love and faith give infinite power to you to create angelic brilliance within your heart and soul.

⁓ epilogue ⌣

We have heard many wonderful stories in this book about the ways in which angels have helped people. Although not everyone will be fortunate enough to meet an angel in person, as you will have seen and experienced in the practical sections of these pages, we can all bring angels closer to us. When working with your angelic guides, let nothing be more important than the quality of your everyday living. It is the commitment that you make to your life that will give you life. If we live in the moment and are true to our highest selves by being kind, compassionate, loving, and trusting, we can be sure that sooner or later we will discover our very own angel forever.

~) acknowledgments (~

We would like to thank the following people for their help, insight, love, trust, and support in making this book possible:

Judith Kendra, Sue Lascelles, Sarah Bennie, Caroline Newbury, David Parrish, Mark Thallander, Christopher Watt, Barbara Moulton, Evelyn Dalton, David Jeans and World Angel Day (www.worldangelday.com), Ross Eckersley, Rachel Eckersley, Edward Potten, Gillian and Michael Smith, Mary Bullough, Greta Woolf, Suzannah James, Janice O'Gara, Rev. Gillian Gordon, Carolyn Burdet, Patty Q., Joan Evans, Stella Morris and staff of Sweeten's Book Shop, Pamela and Roy Cuthbert, David Lomax, Valerie and August Bagarozzi, Emma Heathcote-James, Jacky Newcomb, and Joan Youd.

Finally, our heartfelt thanks go to the contributors, for their generosity in allowing us to include their special stories:

Joan Adamson, the Rev. Beryl Allerton, Saskia van Altena, the Rev. Brian Anderson, Isabel M. Asher, Paul Aynsley, Mary Barnes, Kathy Beauchamp, Connie Benetz, Margaret Bentley, Therese Benzuidenhout, Belinda Bras-Nel, Dawn Carney, Christine Chapman, Melissa Challinor, Jacqueline Christy, Shirley Clark, Brenda Cook, Debe Conway, the Rev. Bill Darlison, Heather Delo, Carol Dickson, Tracy Duke, Karen Eccleston, Maria Gryzlova, Norman

acknowledgments

Hannagen, Irene Hartley, Deb Hollis, Alan Hughes, Louise Hyland, Paula James, Raksha M. Khan, Wendy Lawson, Sean Lucas, Suzannah Newton, Pauline O'Gara, Gwen Owen, Marie Pandolfo, Kate Philips, Lily Philips, Craig Ross, Sue Ross, Stephen Rowen, Maxine Scales, Ralph Shapiro, Jane Simpson, Wan. H. Tonothy, Fiona Williams, and Gaye Young.

~) about the authors (~

Glennyce Eckersley is one of Britain's top researchers on the subject of angels and near-death experiences. She worked in medical research before changing direction to become a member of staff at New Church Theological College, Manchester, where she worked for more than twenty years until leaving in order to pursue her writing on a full-time basis. The author of five best-selling books, which have been translated into several languages, Glennyce lectures internationally and appears regularly on television and radio. She lives in Manchester, England.

Gary Quinn is a leading intuitive spiritual life coach and the founder of Our Living Center. He discovered his own angelic messenger in the Notre Dame cathedral in Paris, at a crucial turning point in his life. He is the best-selling author of *May the Angels Be with You* and *Living in the Spiritual Zone*. He is a popular motivational speaker, in demand worldwide for seminars and events, and frequently appears in the media, both in the United States and in the UK. He lives in Los Angeles.

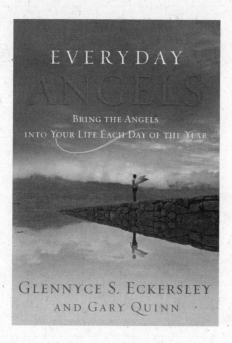